THE QUEST FOR
SELF-DETERMINATION

THE QUEST FOR
SELF-DETERMINATION

Dov Ronen

NEW HAVEN AND LONDON

YALE UNIVERSITY PRESS

1979

Published with assistance from
the Louis Stern Memorial Fund.

Designed by Christopher Harris
and set in Times Roman type
by United Printing Services, Inc., New Haven, Ct.
Printed in the United States of America by
The Vail-Ballou Press, Inc., Binghamton, N.Y.

Published in Great Britain, Europe, Africa, and
Asia (except Japan) by Yale University Press,
Ltd., London. Distributed in Australia and
New Zealand by Book & Film Services, Artarmon,
N.S.W., Australia; and in Japan by
Harper & Row, Publishers, Tokyo Office.

Library of Congress Cataloging in Publication Data

Ronen, Dov.
    The quest for self-determination.

    Bibliography: p.
    Includes index.
    1.   Self-determination, National.
    2.   Minorities—Legal status,
    laws, etc.   I.   Title.
JX4054.R65   341.26   79-11922
                    ISBN 0-300-02364-2

To David, Mihal, and Gili

CONTENTS

PREFACE

"We hold these Truths to be self-evident, that all Men . . . are endowed by their Creator with certain inalienable Rights, that among these are Life, Liberty, and the Pursuit of Happiness . . . that whenever any Form of Government becomes destructive of these Ends, it is the Right of the People to alter or to abolish it, and to institute new Government." With these words the representatives of the thirteen colonies of North America acknowledged the fundamental aspiration of human beings to control their own lives, to be the masters of their own destinies for the attainment of "liberty" and "happiness," that is to enjoy self-determination. This very same quest for self-determination that gave birth to the United States of America reemerged in a new geographical and political setting in the French Revolution.

My thesis in this book is that this fundamental human aspiration, this basic drive, the quest for self-determination, which has appeared locally many times in history, has taken root and spread since the French Revolution to other parts of the world, has been formulated at times in apparently conflicting sets of ideas, has appeared in correspondingly different movements, and has been embodied recently in various documents as a legal right. I will propose here that the quest for self-determination has appeared since the French Revolution in five analytically distinguishable forms, the archetypes of which are nineteenth-century (German, Italian) nationalism, Marxist class struggle, minorities' self-determination associated with the ideas of Woodrow Wilson, anticolonialism, and today's "ethnic" quest for self-determination. This book is thus an interpretation of what I see as past manifestations of the human aspiration to control our own lives, a number of propositions on how these manifestations change, and an assessment of the possible impact of the aspirations on the future.

My aim is to present my thoughts on this subject to the academic world, as well as to the informed public, as clearly, as concisely, and as soon as possible. Thus I do not provide here a review of the relevant literature or of the opinions of noted scholars and political actors, nor do I provide a detailed analysis of a carefully selected sample of cases. I present what may be called a set of philosophical notions and an agenda for further research. My aim has been to understand, to convey, and then to stimulate further debate, even at the price of occasionally departing from conventional scholarly rules.

A few reservations and disclaimers must be stated. As I will repeatedly remind the reader, I use the expression *human being* not, as I have sometimes been understood, "humane being" but in a neutral sense to distinguish *human* beings from other beings. I do not use the term *self-determination* to suggest the "forces of light" against the "forces of darkness" but because I think the term is expressive. I do not mean to encourage movements for self-determination; I observe their presence. I do not propose a specific new world order; I observe that a specific new world order is developing.

I offer these words of caution because I feel that the public in general, and the academic community in particular, may interpret the observation, the diagnosis, and the quite unconventional views presented here as a criticism of existing Western social, political, and economic institutions. I sense, especially in the United States, an inclination, in some circles, to suspect fundamental questions as potentially damaging, to regard new ideas as "utopian" and "unrealistic," and to view the perpetrator as a "dreamer" and "idealist"—all of which are words with negative connotations.

It seems to me that there are at least two reasons for this attitude. First, there may be a latent tendency to balance the almost inevitable, rapidly growing technological change that passes in front of our eyes, as well as our fascination with the implications of technological change for possible encounters of new kinds, against a measure of conservatism, clinging to the status quo in the social, political, and economic spheres. The mind-boggling computer technology, the new horizons of *Star Wars*, the prospects for space travel are projected as being pursued from the customary sociopolitical systems to which we are to return after our fantastic journeys. The uncertainty that this fascinating technological future provides, in the form of robots, unmanned factories, and additional leisure for which we have no precise plan on a mass scale, is more than enough; ideas that forecast a possible shakeup in the sociopolitical sphere, whatever their value, probably seem more than we can handle and still remain sane. The most we ought to be ready for, it is proposed, however reluctantly, is the unknown—and possible undesirable—future impact of technology.

The second reason why the public, including scholars, is not receptive to change in the social, political, and economic system is that the status quo—referred to as democracy, pluralism, or polyarchy—appears to have worked well, and hence questioning is to be resisted. The only new ideas and theories welcomed are those that seem to promise to make the existing systems work better. Other ideas are "simplistic," new- (or old-) "leftist," or worse. That some of the new ideas, or at least the criticism of present ideas, are associated with or drawn from Marxist notions makes the situation worse.

In this book I am not criticizing the quality of any specific system but observing the *perceived* lack of viability, in general, of the modern (nation-)state.* My diagnosis is that pluralism (ethnic pluralism or multinationalism) or, more precisely, the modern

* Here and throughout the book I will use the expressions "modern (nation-)state" and "(nation-)state" to refer to the contemporary political system (of which there are 150 today), instead of "state" which is too general a term and instead of "nation-state" which ought to refer to the very few cases where nation and state overlap.

(nation-)state is seen by people as a less than adequate system, and because of this *perception* the state is under serious attack. An outstanding exception to this rule, today and in the foreseeable future, is the United States, among a few others. The reason for the near uniqueness of the United States is not that it is composed of many ethnic groups, which in turn are composed of descendents of recent immigrants, or that individuals belong to many groups. The reasons for the American exception are that most Americans *perceive* themselves to be freer than any other people on earth, and most Americans *perceive* the American economy as able to provide the goods (food, housing, car, etc.) to which anyone can aspire. The American system is safe from what I will refer to as disintegrative forces as long as this *perception* remains. In those states in many parts of the world where disintegrative forces are active, the sociopolitical framework is *perceived* by sections of populations as incapable of satisfying aspirations to freedoms and goods. The question is not whether pluralism is good or bad but, whatever the system, whether it can provide the positive *perception*. More will be said about this issue later. My purpose here is to state that my diagnosis of the modern (nation-)state stems not from Marxist doctrine or from the view that socialism is ipso facto preferable to an antithetical pluralism or that capitalism is evil (although I do use the words *oppression*, *exploitation*, and the like), but stems instead from my observation that many human beings perceive their freedom, self-determination, and well-being to be limited, which turns them against the pluralist framework.

I have, however, one bias that I wish to confess to at the outset. I believe in the existence of principles—motors of human evolution—and in our obligation to find them. Archimedes said with reference to the lever: "Give me a place to stand, and I will move the earth." I say, give the social sciences a stable point, and they will explain most of the social world. I believe it is one of the duties of the social scientist to search for such a stable point or points. It (or they) may be found one day in propositions based on observation of either human behavior or, as in sociobiology, nonhuman life. I see this study as a minute step in this direction.

A last point. This study is the result of several years of research, reading, innumerable drafts, discussions, and seminars at several academic institutions. But these years are only the academic components. The personal component is probably no less important. It consists of my early life in an East European country, my experiences in the Jewish ghetto and the escape from it that saved my life, life in a kibbutz and in the Israeli Air Force, an interest in the faith of Africans that led me to academic training as an Africanist, and life on four continents. All in all, the perspective from which *The Quest for Self-Determination* was written was not provided by academic experience only but by life experience as well.

My debts therefore reach beyond academia and are owed, in addition to my parents, to the family in the "old country" that saved my life and my family; to Ezer Weitzman, who graciously did not, for good reasons, urge me to stay in the Air Force; to Chaim Perkis, who believed; and to my brother Dan, who was there when I needed support at the start. In the academic sphere my thanks go to my former teachers Professors Benjamin Akzin and Shlomo Avineri, and to colleagues at The Hebrew University, who were patient with me for so many years but probably not patient long enough. Thanks are also owed to the staff and colleagues at the Harry S. Truman Research Institute in Jerusalem; to the Institute I am indebted for the grants that enabled me to carry out research for parts of this book, to Professor Nehemia Levtzion and Dr. Naomi Chazan for their deep friendship, and to Vivienne Kuttner, Reuben Goldman, and Roxana Goldman for their research assistance. Most helpful along the way have been Professors Pierre van den Berghe, Vernon van Dyke, and Michael Weinstein from the University of Washington, University of Iowa, and Purdue University, respectively. The final stages of the research and several drafts were completed at the Center for International Affairs, Harvard University, where I have been a Research Fellow since the 1976–77 academic year. I feel the deepest sense of gratitude to the members and staff of the Center for the stimulating intellectual environment and the effective help they provided; special thanks go to Professors Stanley Hoffmann, Samuel P. Huntington, Herbert Kelman, Joel Migdal, Raymond Vernon, and to Sally Cox, the former executive officer of the Center. I deeply appreciate the assistance of Professor Sidney Verba, who read early versions of the manuscript and was kind enough to invite me to lead with him and with Professors William Schneider and Gary Orren a seminar at the Center that focused on the subject of the book, of Professor Jorge Dominguez for reading various drafts and for comments that helped me to clarify my views, and of the late Professor Rupert Emerson, who read drafts and debated ideas for long hours and encouraged me all along. I wish also to thank now Senator Daniel P. Moynihan, who while a professor at Harvard was kind enough to invite me to assist him in a seminar on "Ethnicity and Politics," and Peter Jacobsohn, editor of the Center, for his guidance.

Many thanks to Marian Neal Ash and the editorial staff of the Yale University Press for their encouragement and help.

Finally, I owe thanks to Naomi, my wife, and to David, Mihal, and Gili, our children, born at different locations in the United States, Africa, and Israel, who probably suffered most through bi- and trilingualism and changes of schools and friends. The blame for all this, including the errors, is mine alone.

Cambridge, Mass.
February 1979

1 SELF-DETERMINATION: AN OVERVIEW

A Look at Recent History

On June 17, 1789, the third estate, six hundred elected commoners representing over 95 percent of the population of France, gathered in Versailles without the other two estates, the nobility and the clergy, and declared themselves the National Assembly. On June 20 the third estate met again and took an oath to continue to press for a new constitution. When, on July 14, a Parisian mob stormed the Bastille, symbol of the repressive old regime, the French Revolution began. In August of the same year the National Assembly passed the Declaration of the Rights of Man and of the Citizen, which proclaimed, among other things, popular sovereignty and the right to resist oppression.

The French Revolution was not the first revolution in human history, but it embodied forcefully the ideas and aspirations of former revolutions, and its impact on institutions and political thought was lasting. By proclaiming the principle of popular sovereignty, the revolution altered the then prevailing conception of the

1

state; the divine right of kings was not only discredited, as it had been in England since the beginning of the eighteenth century, but was also replaced by the divine right of the people.[1]

The revolution in France soon took a different path, away from the ideas promulgated during its early stages, but these ideas spread in the wake of Napoleonic rule and fired nineteenth-century Western Europe with nationalist fervor.

The idea of replacing the time-honored nonrepresentative ruler with popular sovereignty did not, however, offer solutions to the social and economic injustices accentuated by the Industrial Revolution. The eventual elimination of the political oppression of the monarchy and the aristocracy may have provided political freedoms, but there remained what was seen by many as social inequities created by economic exploitation. The fight went on on two fronts: the national fight for political freedom and the social struggle for economic reform.

Political theorists proposed different remedies for man's social and economic ills. Thomas Paine emphasized the need for social as well as political reform. William Godwin attacked private property, social distinctions, marriage, and centralized government. The aristocrat Saint-Simon emphasized the importance of economic organizations in the historical process and proposed the reorganization of the means of production for the benefit of the people as a whole. Charles Fourier urged the organization of small agricultural communities. To achieve a free, just society, Louis Blanc called for state control of all property and economic activity. Pierre Proudhon, the anarchist, opposed private property and favored the establishment of small communities. The English socialist Robert Owen pressed for education and good working conditions. In retrospect, the most prominent of these thinkers was Karl Marx, who proposed the overthrow of the owners of the means of production in order to attain a classless, and therefore a free and equitable, society.

In the 1848 revolutions, the forces that had inherited ideas from the French Revolution and the forces fired by liberal and socialist ideas that sought to remedy the ills of the Industrial Revolution fought, at times together, often in competition, against reactionary rulers in Europe.

The February 1848 revolution in France was, in part, a renewed attempt to achieve the goals of the French Revolution. It restored the republic and introduced a new constitution. In England the revolution took the form of an unsuccessful attempt to revive Chartism, a labor movement pressing for political reform.

In the Austro-Hungarian Empire there was a two-pronged attack on the government of Metternich: in Austria itself the middle class pressed for liberal reforms, while the Magyars and the Czechs rose against their foreign rulers as oppressed minorities.

In the Italian peninsula, Giuseppe Mazzini and Giuseppe Garibaldi led the liberal protest against reactionary rule and the national opposition to Austrian rule in Lombardy and Venice.

In Germany the 1848 revolution strove for both liberal reforms and national liberation in the form of German unification. Uprisings in various parts of the German Confederation and street fighting in Berlin gave way to an elected national assembly that met on May 18 in Frankfurt to push for both aims.

The 1848 revolutions did not fully succeed in bringing about either radical social change or national unification. Countervailing reactionary political forces proved stronger. The unification of Italy did not come until 1861 and that of Germany until 1871. But the ideas—both those stemming from the French Revolution and those emerging in the wake of the Industrial Revolution—persisted, gained strength, and spread.

On the social reform front, the newly constituted or strengthened assemblies or parliaments in Germany, Italy, Austria, and elsewhere worked for more liberal legislation. The struggle for more radical reforms was, however, borne by the Socialist and Marxist movements. Marxist doctrine, launched in the *Communist Manifesto* only in 1848—the year of revolutions—rapidly gained strength, culminating in the 1917 October Revolution in Russia.

The ideas of the French Revolution—translated now into nationalist movements—proceeded to sweep through Central and Eastern Europe. Slav nationalism arose in the Austro-Hungarian Empire and in the Balkans. The ferocious suppression in 1876 of the Bulgarian revolution against the Turks prompted Serbians and Montenegrins to go to war against Turkey. The result was the independence of Serbia, Montenegro, Rumania, and Bulgaria. There also emerged secret societies, such as Union or Death, which aimed at the national unification of the southern Slavs (Yugoslavs). A member of this organization, Gavrilo Princip, assassinated the heir to the Austrian throne, Archduke Francis Ferdinand, which precipitated World War I.

The principle of popular sovereignty, expressed as the right of self-determination, was widely recognized by the end of World War I. Self-determination was not only a declared war aim of the Allies toward the end of the war—President Wilson being its most illustrious spokesman—but it was also held as a guiding principle by the Germans, the Italians, and the Bolsheviks. Commitment to the principle was not rooted in idealism in all cases but was in some instances a calculated policy intended to make its spokesmen appear as champions of the restless minorities. The post-World War I peace treaties fell far short of implementing in full the highly regarded principle, but the founding of the League of Nations and the granting of independence to Czechoslovakia, Hungary, Poland, Yugoslavia, Armenia, Finland, Estonia, Latvia, and Lithuania were important steps. One may also add the struggle of the Irish against English domination, the separation of Northern Ireland from the independent republic of Ireland in 1921, and the granting of limited self-government to India in 1919. Responding to nationalist pressures from various parts of the Empire, Britain also freed the dominions—Australia, Canada, and New Zealand—which became autonomous members of the Commonwealth in 1931. From that date on, no legislation in the British Parliament would be binding on the dominions without their consent.

Political use of the principle of self-determination did not end with World War I. Hitler's occupation of the Rhineland in 1936 and of Austria and Czechoslovakia in 1938 was carried out under the pretext of unifying all Germans in the name of self-determination. At the Munich Conference of September 1938, Britain (represented by Chamberlain), France (represented by Daladier), Italy (represented by Mussolini), and Germany (represented by Hitler) agreed on the German occupation of the Sudetenland, a predominantly German-speaking part of Czechoslovakia, in the name of the people's right to self-determination. Up to the occupation of the Sudetenland, Hitler's aggression was seen by many as the completion of the unfinished business of reorganizing the boundaries of Europe. Only when Hitler occupied the entire Czechoslovak state, including sections that did not have German majorities, did the politicians, and Europeans in general, awaken to the realities of Hitler's scheme. But it should be noted that for the purpose of aligning public opinion behind him, at least at home, Hitler invaded Czechoslovakia under the pretext of safeguarding the interests of German minorities, and marched into Poland in 1939 in order to secure Danzig and the Polish Corridor, both predominantly German in population. The principle of sovereignty of the people—modified from the original idea born in the French Revolution and appearing now as national self-determination—still prevailed in the minds of people on the eve of World War II and, in still different forms, afterward.

The Atlantic Charter, signed by fifteen representatives of governments in September 1941, reaffirmed the commitment to self-determination. On January 1, 1942, representatives of twenty-six governments, some of them governments-in-exile, signed the Declaration of the United Nations. The Charter of the United Nations, the Covenants on Human Rights, the Declaration on the Granting of Independence to Colonial Countries and Peoples (General Assembly Resolution 1514 [XV], 14 December 1960), the Declaration on Principles of International Law Concerning Friendly Relations and Co-operation among States (Resolution 2625 [XXV] of 24 October 1970), and a host of other declarations revive and recognize people's right to self-determination.[2] Unlike those following World War I, these declarations were specifically aimed at colonized countries. Under the principle of a people's right to fight against colonial rule, ten new states had been born in Asia by 1955 (India, Pakistan, Ceylon, the Philippine Republic, Vietnam, Cambodia, Laos, Burma, Korea, and Indonesia), and the successive independence of scores of new African states began in 1957. Decolonization has shown that the right to self-determination is not restricted to one race, not based on the size or economic and political preparedness of a group, nor even on a common culture or common history—but first of all on the human right not to be ruled by other peoples.

The United Nations documents speak of the right of *peoles* to self-determination, implying colonized peoples. They specifically support the territorial integrity of existing states. But Biafra's attempt to become independent, the Eritrean efforts to do the same, the separatist movement in Quebec, the drive for autonomy in Scotland, and the Muslims' drive for independence from the Philippines are only a few indications that the struggle for self-determination that began in the French Revolution has not stopped. These contemporary cases relate back to the idea promulgated in the French Revolution; they are the latest phase in an ongoing quest.

The Thesis in Brief

While the age of self-determination was born in the French Revolution, it had been in the womb of history long before; men of action contributed to its multidirectional development, and a long line of philosophers enhanced its intellectual stature. Since the French Revolution, the idea has spread throughout the world, unifying peoples into nations, prompting revolutions, crumbling empires, freeing colonies, and threatening modern states. We are still in the midst of a spreading quest for self-determination, and the end is not yet in sight.

Self-determination is laid down as a right in various documents, as popular sovereignty in the Declaration of the Rights of Man and of the Citizen and as "peoples' " right to self-determination in the Charter of the United Nations. It is variously defined and interpreted. Neither written words nor official interpretations, however, motivate people to seek self-determination; they are merely instrumental in spreading it. When a political leader speaks of the right to self-determination for his "people," he refers not to the legal term but to the *idea* of an "inalienable right" to freedom from "them." This idea lies at the root of the struggle.

The nobility of the idea does not guarantee nobility of action. "People" fighting for their own "freedom" and self-determination have oppressed other people probably as often and as harshly as those motivated by "evil" ideas. The Napoleonic wars were the first to demonstrate that. By pointing to the "right of self-determination" as a motivating force, my intention is not to enlist sympathy and support for the "oppressed." My argument is that this "right" is an expression, in succinct form, of the aspiration to rule one's self and to not be ruled by others. This aspiration, perhaps a basic human motivation, was written in the American Declaration of Independence and became a motivating force with eventual universal applicability in the French Revolution. In other words, my contention is that within the context of the seventeenth and eighteenth centuries, what may be a basic human motivation emerged, for good or for bad, as a sociopolitical force and has been spreading since then.

Whatever the local circumstances may be, I believe that during the last two hundred years or so the quest for self-determination has epitomized the aspiration of human beings to be "free," or to be "free from" what they perceive as "others." Narrowly conceived, self-determination is the control of one's self; this control is seen not merely as freedom, but as a positive human condition, or the prerequisite for a positive human condition, for the "good life," self-fulfillment, and the like. This is not a definition of self-determination; it is an interpretation of the *idea* of self-determination held by those pursuing it. In recent history, for example, sections of populations in colonized countries expected that freedom from colonial rule would bring improvement in conditions of life in general, including a rise in the standard of living.

The French Revolution was a turning point in human history, for it symbolized the recognition of the right of the "ruled," as such, to turn against the "rulers." Throughout human history numerous uprisings have occurred, but not before the French Revolution, not even in the aftermath of the American Declaration of Independence, did the idea of the right to self-determination take root. The change is not because of the French Revolution per se, which merely symbolizes it, but because of the stage at which the evolution of the idea of *human freedom* had arrived in that period.

The idea of self-determination could not have been born without the secularizing spirit of the eighteenth century, which freed the minds of *individuals* from the bondage of institutional religion. Consequently, my thesis is that the "self" in self-determination is the singular, individual human being and not any aggregation of human beings. The quest for self-determination, at its core, is not a national or any other group aspiration, but the aspiration of the individual human being to the vague notions of "freedom" and "the good life." It is only because the institutionalization of individual self-determination is not (or not yet) possible that the *aggregation* of "I's," the "us," is substituted. But each aggregation is only a temporary "us," because it does not, cannot, provide self-determination for each "I." The aggregation splits into a new "us" and "them" and becomes the stage for a new drive for self-determination, fueled by the hope that after freedom from "them," *my* self-determination will be realized. Because the new "us" often becomes just another framework that appears to limit the freedom of the individual, of the real "self," the perception of a new "them" is prompted, and hence the formation of a new "us," for the further pursuit of the aspired-to "freedom" and "good life." And so a new quest for self-determination evolves, with another new "us"; and then another, possibly ad infinitum.

But legitimate questions arise. Are there not objectively defined nations, ethnic groups, linguistic groups, religious groups, and the like that are *given* communities of "us"? From time to time do not such groups rise in nationalistic fervor? Have we not witnessed the rise of the Germans, the Nigerians, the Scots, and so on? The answer is: Yes and No. Yes, these groups have existed for various lengths of time. But it is the self-perception by individual human beings of themselves as Germans, Nigerians, and Scots, prompted by the perception of "them" (primarily the French, the colonizer British, and the English, respectively) that has *activated* these groups of "us."[3] Human beings speaking a certain language, guided by similar values, and relating to an historical past have always existed, but only when threatening neighbors or rulers, who may not speak the same language or relate to the same historical past, are perceived as "them" or "others" is an "us" born. To switch to the contemporary scene, it is not the ethnic groups that disrupt national unity, but the perceived absence of national unity, the perception of "them," that creates the ethnic groups. One's religion, mother tongue, culture, also one's education, class, sex, skin color, even one's height, age, and family situation are all potentially unifying factors. Each factor can also be ignored as irrelevant in the formation of an "us." Various unifying factors, such as language, religion, and color of skin, seem "natural." I propose that none is. Language, culture, a real or assumed historical origin, and religion form identities for an "us" in our minds; and only so long as they exist in our minds as unifying factors do the entities of "us" persist. Until future research proves otherwise, we ought to take for granted only two basic human entities: individuals and all humanity. All entities between these two, save a mother and a newborn child, are arbitrary formations created by our perception of ourselves vis-à-vis others.

Toward a Classification

Since the French Revolution, the human quest for self-determination has appeared in five different manifestations.[4] The French Revolution produced the Declaration of the Rights of Man and of the Citizen, reflecting in part Rousseau's ideas about freedom, and demoted the nobility, who were believed to be the obstacle to the realization of a society of free men. However, industrialization and the rise of capitalism convinced many thinkers, including Karl Marx, that abolition of the nobility was not enough. Marx, whose ideas were more influential than those of others of his time who held similar views, argued that the alienation of man was caused by property, and he urged aggregation around *class* identity as a means to ameliorate the human condition. Nevertheless, the emergence of unification movements in Germany and Italy in reaction to Napoleonic rule activated *national* identity to compete later with the Marxist notion of self-determination through class identity. In the 1848 revolutions throughout Europe, language, culture, and/or common history provided a more effective identity than class identity, in part because Marx's teachings were little known then; but both helped to disrupt Europe toward the end of the nineteenth century and at the beginning of the twentieth. The third type of quest for self-determination, the *national-minorities* identity, was adopted by President Wilson as the appropriate means of achieving self-determination in Europe; later Wilson used it to combat Lenin's clever move to support national movements along with the *class* struggle. Between the two world wars, muted efforts for self-determination by various peoples continued but were overwhelmed by power politics, by the failure of the League of Nations to respond to the crises in Manchuria in 1931 and in Ethiopia in 1935, and, finally, by the death of the League of Nations, which had been created, in part, to promote Wilsonian self-determination.

Wilson and Marx (and later Lenin) proposed basically similar ideas: the right of self-determination in the face of perceived oppression. Although one proposed national minorities' identity and the other class identity, both recognized the right of people to rise against the perceived oppressiveness of the political system. Marx proposed a classless homogeneous society; Wilson, a nationally homogeneous one. Marx considered national divisions irrelevant in constructing a better society; Wilson thought class divisions insignificant. Both were right. National and class divisions are unimportant until we make them relevant. And so it is with any other divisions within humanity. We are all human beings, whatever our color, sex, age, occupation, religion, language group, weight, height, intelligence—definable as human beings different from other species. Our identities are, in themselves, irrelevant for social distinctions until we make them relevant. We identified black people as Negroes, whatever their age, religion, occupation, capabilities, or self-identities. Then the tables were turned, and *they* said, "Yes, I *am* a Negro, but let's make this as clear as possible by translating it into English and making the dichotomy clear: You are *white*; I am *black*." Dark-skinned human beings, the same as others, *make* one of their identities (poor, American, blue-collar, man or woman, southerner, etc.) relevant as a weapon in their fight for their individual self-determination.

After World War II, the division of Europe into spheres of influence by the major powers and the economic poverty of the Euro-

pean victors muted for a while movements of self-determination in
Europe and amplified efforts for economic reconstruction.[5] The
quest for self-determination shifted to the third world, where a
fourth type of self-determination, the non-European, or non-
white/"racial," quest for self-determination, already present among
blacks in the United States, emerged to terminate colonial rule. In
the first phase of their struggle, mainly between the two wars, Africans and Asians fought for human rights, equal rights within the
colonial system, the same as Frenchmen or Englishmen had. They
did not then fully activate their non-European/racial identity in a
quest for *self-determination* from colonial rule, but in general
fought for more political rights within the colonial framework.
Only after World War II did colonial rule itself become an
unacceptable form of subordination, even though greater political
rights were then granted. The exercise of the right to terminate the
unacceptable colonial rule was almost completed by the 1960s. The
quest for self-determination was carried on without considera-
tion—as it was deemed irrelevant—of the economic viability of the
emerging states, but with the hope of supporting individual personal freedom and the "good life."

Decolonization was probably the most effective universalizer
of the idea of self-determination of all five historical types, because it affected large numbers of peoples and because it made self-
determination relevant to new types of aggregations. Decolonization has shown that size of a country, economic viability, and
European origin or white race are not prerequisites for the right to
self-determination. Decolonization has not only effected further
pressures for decolonization, as in southern Africa, but also
influenced, at least indirectly, the rise of the fifth type of self-determination: *ethnic* (encompassing, roughly, linguistic, religious,
historical, cultural) self-determination. The Scottish demand for
self-government, the Eritrean secession attempt, the independence
of Bangla Desh, the Quebec drive for autonomy, and Bougain-
ville's demand for separation from Papua New Guinea are representative of a long list of cases of ethnic self-determination on
five continents.

This fifth, contemporary quest for self-determination differs from the other quests for self-determination in three ways:

1. The cases emerge in sovereign (nation-)states where popular political participation, the democratic process, has at least been introduced, exists, or is adhered to in principle if not in practice. Thus, the Magyar quest for self-determination in Austro-Hungary is not classified here as an ethnic quest for self-determination, while the Biafran fight in Nigeria is.

2. The groups of people seeking self-determination identify themselves on the basis of linguistic, historical, or general cultural identities, which have never been totally ignored but have been relegated to a "subgroup" status within the (nation-)state. These self-identities we commonly term *ethnicity*; hence, this type of self-determination may conveniently, although not always accurately, be called *ethnic* self-determination.

3. This type of self-determination, in contrast to national self-determination, is centripetal (tends toward the individual as the center) rather than centrifugal, disintegrates rather than integrates into the state, disunites rather than unites diversities, and tends toward the smaller rather than the larger.

The relatively muted, scant efforts to achieve self-determination prior to the second half of the 1960s indicate that people had been willing to try to make it *within* the political entities of which they were a part. Feeling they have failed, they are now trying to make it as a separate community within *or* outside of the existing political entity. Because absolute individual freedom is impossible, a limited amount of subordination of man by man may be necessary for orderly public life. Contemporary quests for ethnic self-determination, however, raise doubts whether the modern (nation-)state (steered by the mechanisms of democracy or not) is, today, the optimal framework to provide, in every case, the minimal pattern and degree of subordination that each and every human being would call "freedom." The quests for ethnic self-determination in Quebec, Biafra, Scotland, Bangla Desh, and elsewhere indicate that for some groups the pattern of subordination provided by their modern states is unacceptable.

Ethnic versus Class Identity

The five types of quest for self-determination—national, class, minorities, non-European/racial, and ethnic—succeeded each other as dominant types from the nineteenth century to the latter part of the twentieth. However, a new type does not eliminate previously dominant types. All five types exist today in different parts of the world: the emergence of the Palestinians is an example of the feeling of national identity; class rather than ethnic identity is exhibited by peoples in Brittany and parts of Italy, for example; Catholics in Northern Ireland and native Americans in the United States feel a minorities' identity; blacks in South Africa and to an extent in Rhodesia show a non-European/racial identity; and in scores of states, as I will show in Chapter 2, ethnic identity appears.

Furthermore, two or more identities may be present in the same political framework at the same time. In her quest for self-determination, a black woman in the United States may now claim her identity as a woman, her identity as a black, or both. Class identity and ethnic identity, however, are probably the most prominent competing identities today, but because of social mobility, class identity is successfully being replaced by ethnic identity, which has long, if not always, been an available option. In France and in Italy this switch from class to ethnic identity is not complete, as evidenced by the strength of their Socialist and Communist parties.

The switch from one identity to another is possible because all identities are optional weapons in quests for self-determination. Those who use class identity and ethnic identity against the state, government, or "establishment" perceive the issue as unacceptable "subordination," "domination," or "exploitation" by "them." In both cases, the intensity may be mute or revolutionary; ethnic movements, as well as Marxist movements, have their "socialists" and their "communists."

Both movements are politically "dangerous," because they are motivated by opposition to the center. A very important difference, however, between the class and ethnic movements, which both seek liberation from oppression by "them," is that the former is usually not territory bound, while the latter often is. For this reason, the class cannot and does not claim to be a separate and distinct people; the ethnic group can and often does. Thus, a class aims at changing the *regime* of the state to create a community of all of "us" under the dictatorship of the proletariat; while an ethnic group aims at changing the *framework* of the state and demands a separate state or, at least, at times only as a temporary claim, autonomous status within the state.

Another factor facilitates the switch from class to ethnic identity and vice versa. In the nineteenth century and early twentieth, political grievances against the state and the ruler could be separated from economic grievances against the nobility and the emerging capitalist class. Today, both types of grievances can be, and are, directed against the state and its rulers. The modern state, whether as a welfare state or state that has nationalized private property, is held responsible not only for political freedom, representation, and rights, but also for the economic well-being of its inhabitants. Thus, the ideas that originated in the French Revolution and the ideas aimed at solving economic problems created by the Industrial Revolution now have a common target: the modern (nation-)state.

Self-Determination and the State

Because of the apparent or actual impossibility of institutionalizing complete personal freedom in an all-encompassing social framework, the ongoing quest for self-determination creates political frameworks, which have multiplied from the eighteenth century to our day. Again, it is not the purpose of the quest for ethnic self-determination to create more or smaller states. Human beings aggregating around their ethnic identity struggle to control their own lives, to escape domination by what *they* consider "others." The *result* of the effort is a pressure toward secession and new states.

If such an interpretation of the quest for self-determination is correct, then in the remainder of this century pressure for the creation of possibly hundreds of new states is probable, unless a new world order is born to satisfy the quest for self-determination without secession.

In chapter 5 I will try to analyze forces that may shape a future world order. But let us assume that the tendency toward multiplication of states continues, as it has during the last two hundred years, and that this multiplication of states will not affect the character of the modern state. Why not hundreds of states? Is a significant increase in smaller political entities a reductio ad absurdum of the right to self-determination?[6] Would such a trend be, by definition, a negative, destructive change from an existing positive, constructive situation? What is the validity of the right to self-determination (implying also the right of secession) vis-à-vis the territorial integrity of sovereign states? Today some one hundred and fifty independent states provide political frameworks for some four billion human beings. What does this sovereign independent statehood mean today?

First of all, it means that the major chunk of the earth's land surface is subdivided into some one hundred and fifty territorial units that we call (nation-)states. There are a few exceptions to this rule: for example, Namibia (Southwest Africa) is not yet an independent state. But the principle is that states are a certain number of territorially bound entities. Second, every independent state has a government of one form or another that is at least the ultimate arbiter of affairs within the state. The well-known rule of noninterference in the affairs of a state also means that the power and authority of the state and its government (or governments in federal systems) over the citizens of that state are not limited by any outside authority or power. The few limitations on this *un*limited authority, by international law and conventions, are ratified, consented to, by the state's government and, for all practical purposes, may be annulled at any time. Third, independent statehood implies an economic entity; the state has a budget and trade relations with other states; it regulates, if it wishes, income, taxes, employment, and welfare benefits; and it has rights over the natural resources of its territory. Fourth, independent statehood implies, but does not always achieve, a cultural identity. Here the word *culture* means a set of customs and values. Culture, furthermore, is often a major building block of the (nation-)state. Fifth, independent statehood implies a formally equal status in the international scene, entailing in principle one vote in international forums regardless of size, power, and other factors. Also, as the chief representatives of their states, all heads of state have equal legal status internationally, regardless of who they are or how they became heads of state.

These five points seem the most important characteristics of independent modern states: territoriality, sovereignty (implying exclusive right to the use of power), economic control (including property rights over material resources), assumed cultural identity, and equal international status. Now most people, including political scientists and historians, hold that (nation-)states are the modern political frameworks, and whatever change and development are necessary in the future will come about *within* and *among* them. In short, the modern (nation-)state is accepted de facto, de jure, and, if I may add, de ratio.

There is reason for this stand. First and foremost, most nonindependent people aspire to independent statehood, an indication of its status and appeal. Second, between the images of the primitive tribe of the distant past and the present modern state stretches an ascending line from simplicity to complexity, from traditional to modern, from primary relations to secondary relations; in short, we tend to see a progression from a ''lower'' to a ''higher'' quality of human relations. Third, the modern state provides the needed security for its inhabitants. Fourth, in recent history the modern state has facilitated economic activities leading to higher technology and, thus, to a higher standard of living. For these reasons alone, the present international system is deemed worthy of preservation.

Furthermore, for at least four reasons, separatist tendencies are viewed negatively. First, we think positively of the term *integration*, for it connotes oneness, and negatively of the term *disintegration*, which implies disorder and chaos.

Second, we hold that ''breaking away'' would create a too small, economically nonviable, entity. We hold this to be so in spite of the apparent evidence that there is probably no correlation between state size, population size, and economic viability.

Third, ideological overtones often influence our judgment. The separatists in many instances use Marxist slogans and/or turn to the Soviet Union or China for tangible support. The Eritreans, who have claimed as their homeland the strategically important land strip on the shores of the Red Sea, are reported to have received support, including arms, from Cuba and the Soviet Union. Views toward their claim have been based not so much on the substantive issue of their quest for self-determination as on the ideological factor. (It should be noted that the Eritrean movement fought as determinedly against the Ethiopia of Haile Selassie as against the Ethiopia of the present self-proclaimed Marxist military regime.)

Fourth and last, we regard tendencies toward disintegration as exceptions to the rule of an otherwise successful integration process. In Europe, integration within states has, we think, been accomplished after centuries of trial and error; in the third world we are witnessing, in the words Daniel Lerner used in the title of a book, "The Passing of Traditional Society."[7] The general trend, since it seems successful and positive, receives our support; the exception, our condemnation. The many movements seeking ethnic self-determination in Western Europe alone show that such assessment of European states' integration is questionable.

It is difficult to marshal arguments against these reasons except to say that they may hide more than they reveal, emphasize appearance and not substance, and possibly reflect questionable preferences. First of all, most nonindependent peoples probably aspire to independent statehood not because it is "good" per se but because the modern state is the *only* legitimate (and also prestigious) political entity available. Colonized people aspire, when they do, to freedom from colonial rule, and people in general aspire, when they do, to freedom from *perceived oppression*, and *then* to independent statehood, for the state is the existing legal, accepted framework for providing freedom. Second, the modern state may be deemed the crown of human political achievement, as a complex entity, only if the consolidation of the results of warfare, conflict, and historical accidents are credited as a human achievement. Most states' boundaries were established in war (some African states' boundaries were drawn on the map of the continent) and were often consolidated by historical accidents. Third, the statement that the state provides the security of the people is inversely put. Commonly it is the people, the armed forces and, not least, civilians, who provide security for the integrity and continued existence of the *state*. It is not states and humanless armies that fight, but human beings. So, at best, *some* human beings provide security for other human beings and a *sense* of security for themselves. Furthermore, it is doubtful that modern states provide more internal security than primitive states. Modern states, not primitive political systems, have high rates of most types of crime. Still, people *think* that the state provides security. Fourth, there is some awareness today in certain sections of populations that higher technology and even a higher standard of living are not necessarily positive values. For various reasons, many draw away from what modernity or development entail. Existing states therefore cannot necessarily be seen in a positive light as providing conditions for complex economic activities and high technology.

But all the above probably circles around value judgments that will hardly be shared by everyone. More convincing, perhaps, is the argument that if existing states are considered the ultimate political entities—a pinnacle of human achievement to be taken as a given, nonalterable fact—then every process, institution, and attitude of their inhabitants, including quests for ethnic self-determination, ought to be fitted, one way or another, to the state. If, however, the state is *not* considered the terminal entity, but alterable then *the state as a political entity may be liable to be changed and molded to fit the wishes of its citizens*, especially to accommodate quests for ethnic self-determination.

Today the first statement is generally held to be valid. General public and political practitioners apart, if there is anything common to most (if not all) of the social science literature on development, modernization, self-determination, and ethnic conflict, it is the acceptance of the existing framework of states and the state system. Gabriel Almond, Sidney Verba, Samuel Huntington, Karl Deutsch, James Coleman, Arnold Rivkin, Fred Riggs, Lucien Pye,

David Apter, and a long list of other noted scholars all appear to hold this position, explicitly or not. As recent a work as Crawford Young's *The Politics of Cultural Pluralism*, which emphasizes, with a long list of examples, the evident schisms in existing states, concludes that the state is here to stay:

Nation-building can only move forward through an ongoing consociational bargaining and compromise. There is simply no escape from the existing state system, as the political frame within which mankind must seek a better life. . . . The sensitive application of wisdom accumulated in the observation of the politics of cultural pluralism is not beyond the reach of statesmanship. There is, of course, no other choice.[8]

The terminology (or jargon) of the same literature also takes the state as a given: nation building, state building, nationalism, civic culture, mobilization, institutionalization of political organizations of the political system, input-output, aid to the state, national integration, centralization or decentralization of power are just a few of these terms. The approach in scholarly writings has been that everything—loyalties, culture, attitudes, interests, values, family, economic structure, and systems—is to be molded to the framework of the state.

The few, infrequent deviations from this approach are ignored or considered irrelevant. The primary deviant is the Marxist. The state as a legitimate and appropriate political entity has been questioned by Marx and his successors and has been expected to "wither away." But for Marxists the disappearance of the state is at best the *outcome* of changing relations concerning the means of production—the regime—within the state, which Marxists as well as the social scientists feel is here to stay, at least for a while.

Searching for non-Marxist deviating views, one could probably go back as far as Plato and Aristotle, who spoke of the *polis* and not of the heterogeneous state of today, or to Rousseau, who favored the city-state of Geneva. More recently, Alfred Cobban stated:

At different times different institutions have embodied the political ideals of man. We need not here pass judgment on the historic process which has at one time fixed men's hearts on the city or the nation, at another on a civilization or an empire. The truth is that while loyalty to the community in which for the time being are enshrined the highest aspirations of social organization is a perennial quality in human nature, the object of that loyalty has varied widely from age to age. There is little to suggest that the combination of cultural and political unity in the idea of the nation state is the last, or that it is the highest, of those mortal gods to which men have sometimes paid undue adoration.[9]

Still more recently, Cynthia H. Enloe has questioned whether the nation-state is the appropriate framework for development:

Most political scientists are sensitive to the pitfalls of American and democratic assumptions and try to guard against them in comparative studies. However, a basic nation-state bias persists. It relegates ethnic groups to the status of dependent variables or policy problems. The danger is that, in assuming the nation-state to be natural and the national elite's problems to be the primary challenges for development, the outside observer implies that integration and assimilation are by definition good.[10]

Scholars who hold the view that the nation-state is not the terminal political entity, that a political system, in all its respects, has to fit human beings and not vice versa, are few and far between.

Nevertheless, the pressures of ethnic self-determination will probably continue, possibly producing an enormous proliferation of political entities, perhaps in the hundreds, with implications for the international system. As I said earlier, such an eventuality might seem farfetched, but possibly no more than the eventuality to a hypothetical observer at the Congress of Vienna in 1815 that fifty states would be equal members in the United Nations of 1945, or (to show the faster rate of change) the eventuality to an observer at the United Nations in 1945 that one hundred and fifty independent states would be members of this body in 1979. As I have tried to show above, this growth has resulted from quests for self-determination. In any case, attempts to block the quest for self-determination will continue, and political leaders *and* scholars will understandably search for measures to contain "disintegrating tendencies" and to regulate "ethnic conflicts" by various means.[11]

Other factors, however, will foster the multiplication of political entities by the breaking up of existing states or their reorganization into new types of modern states and hence into a new world order. One factor is the very aspiration toward more ethnically homogeneous entities, a philosophy akin to the environmentalist's "small is beautiful." This will tend toward the revival of local folklore and custom, to populism, communalism, and other social, ideological, and pseudoideological trends around the world.

A second factor is the growing support for human rights and its extension to the right of self-determination. Today the preponderant, scholarly view is that the right to self-determination is not limited to colonized peoples. Negative reactions of the Organization of African Unity and the United Nations to the quest for self-determination in already independent states is often based on the possible epidemic effect of such aspirations rather than on any overt denial of the right of self-determination.

These two factors, however, are not sufficient in themselves to disrupt the existing international system of states overnight. The countervailing forces are much stronger. Furthermore, no alternative—at least no better alternative—yet exists or is visualized. But the question is not whether the modern state should wither away or be replaced by other forms of political entities. The point is that we are living in age when growing numbers of human beings in different parts of the world aspire to self-determination. In its present stage the struggle for self-determination in its full sway threatens the unity of the state, as the cases of Quebec, Eritrea, the Basques, and others prove. In most cases, this threat to break away is not initially intentional; more often than not there is no single-minded aim to separate, but in practically all cases, efforts within an already independent state to be "free" tend toward such a breakup.

I have tried to argue in this chapter that what we label nationalism, Marxism, Wilsonian self-determination, African and Asian decolonization, and subnationalism (or ethnonationalism) are successive dominant manifestations of the quest for self-determination that originated in the French Revolution. These manifestations

were: national self-determination, class self-determination, minorities self-determination, non-European/racial self-determination, and
ethnic self-determination. The quest for self-determination, an *idea*
connoting freedom and not a legal term, is basically an individual
quest. Because of the lack of conceptualization and the improbabil-
ity of realizing individual "freedom" alone, human beings seek
communities of "us." The five different types of quests are the result of the activation of one of several identities human beings have
into communities of "us" vis-à-vis a perceived "them." The resulting community of "us" creates new perceptions of "them" and
the activation of a new identity to confront "them," and so on. The
quest for self-determination is therefore ongoing and probably inter-
minable.

At present, ethnic self-determination is dominant, and its
emergence threatens "disintegration" or breakup of the so-called
modern (nation-)state. This trend is deemed negative, because the
modern (nation-)state is seen as a positive political achievement;
any threat to it is to be resisted. I have suggested that the modern
state and the one hundred and fifty state systems are not necessarily positive and final and that they are bending to the pressure of
ethnic self-determination.

The outcome of ethnic quests for self-determination will
probably not be complete secession but a new type of relationship
between ethnic entities and the frameworks of which they are now
part. We may call it a new type of federation in which the wider
economic entity provides a framework for sociopolitically independent entities. Complete independence in a fully sovereign state
is the declared aim of ethnic secessionists because there is no other
institutional system toward which to aim. What future pressures
may bring about is a new type of institution that will provide a
sense of self-determination and retain the economic framework to
make self-determination economically feasible. Thus, when the
leaders of the Parti Quebecois say: "We are dissatisfied with the
status quo, and we want independence," and the Ottawa government says: "We agree to change the status quo because we realize
that it is unsatisfactory, but we want to preserve Canada," they are
ultimately saying the same thing. The one says the cup is half full,

the other that the cup is half empty. Quebec may have its independence in the sociopolitical entity to which it aspires, and Ottawa may preserve Canada as an economic entity to which it aspires.

Conventional terms—autonomy, self-rule, federation, decentralization, devolution, and so on—are unsatisfactory, although the ultimate arrangements may not be far from the meaning of any of these terms. The terms are not satisfactory, because they connote *administrative* measures, when the issue is sentimental, emotional, patriotic, national. People in quest of self-determination are willing to accept less autonomy with more flag, but not vice versa.

2 THE FIVE MANIFESTATIONS

The political awakening in the eighteenth century sought the complete liberation of the human being. Up to the period of the French Revolution, the idea that man has a right to be free had few proponents. Since then, despite several setbacks, the idea of the right to self-determination has spread, transmitted by modernization and improved communications and strengthened by the cataclysmic impact of the two world wars.[1]

The intellectual fathers of this awakening were Locke, Rousseau, and other philosophers of the Englightenment. Locke supported inalienable individual rights and limited government. He emphasized that individual man, not the national group, was the repository of all rights; popular sovereignty could be linked to *any* aggregation of individuals. Rousseau searched for a way to free people from the authority of the state, which, in his opinion, lacked legitimate political authority. Rousseau raised the individual as the object of liberation. He did not elevate the general will to an independent moral entity transcending the individual, but said the general will *is* the will of individuals.[2] He believed, as "Kant [did] after him, that freedom consisted in obedience to laws which men imposed upon themselves," for Rousseau believed that man wants

24

"to obey himself alone."[3] Only later did "general will" become a synonym for "national will"; Rousseau did not mean them to be synonymous, but to a person "who read his own national group into Rousseau's reference to *the people*, that guiding force of society which Rousseau termed the *general will* became merely a synonym for the national will."[4]

Rousseau "was in no sense a nationalist,"[5] although nationalism later did emerge, with Rousseau as its spiritual father. He aimed at individual freedom, although he lacked the "intellectual penetration" clearly to convey the idea.[6] The storm of the French Revolution aborted individual freedom. As Max Stirner said:

Not individual man . . . has been emancipated: it is merely the citizen, the *citoyen*, political man that has been liberated; and he is not real man, but just an example of the human species, to be more precise, of the genus *citoyen*. It is only as such, not as man, that he has been liberated. In the French Revolution it is not the individual that is world-historically active, only the nation.[7]

The French Revolution promulgated individual self-determination, not national self-determination. Locke, Rousseau, and the thinkers of the French Revolution sought *human* rights, the rights of the nonrulers. Neither did they aim at group rights of nation, ethnic group, or class; they aimed at the rights of the individual human being. Nationalism *becomes* a collective expression of the individual yearning for freedom; the nation-state is seen as a political framework that will reconcile the impossibility of full individual freedom by the democratically expressed will of its individual citizens. The precise term, therefore, for the opposition to alien rule, to being ruled by "them," is not nationalism, but *self-determination* (or the quest for self-determination).[8] *National* self-determination—the term used by Wilson, Lenin, and commonly by scholars—is merely a type of self-determination.

Five types of quests for self-determination have been dominant, at successive periods, between the French Revolution and the present: mid-nineteenth-century European national self-determination; late-nineteenth-century Marxist class self-determination; post-

Table 1.   The Five Manifestations of Self-Determination[a]

LABEL REFERENCE	TYPE	DOMINANT PERIOD	MAIN GEOGRAPHIC LOCATION
1. nationalism	national self-determination	1830s to 1880s	Europe
2. Marxism	class[b] self-determination	mid-nineteenth century	Europe plus
3. Wilsonian self-determination	minorities' self-determination	1916 to 1920s	Eastern Europe
4. decolonization	racial[c] self-determination	(1945) to 1960s	Africa and Asia
5. ethnonationalism or subnationalism	ethnic self-determination	mid-1960s–	Africa, Asia, Europe, North America, Far East

a. The categories are not airtight or exclusive; they are presented for purposes of orientation only.

b. The term *class* is borrowed from the Marxist terminology, but not necessarily in conformity with his definition. The support of Communist and Socialist parties, for instance, is taken as quests for class self-determination. The emphasis here, as throughout the study, is on the subjective view, not on the objective condition of participants.

c. "Racial" or "pigmentational" or, simply, "non-European." The use here is in a political context, referring to the African, Asian, Arab, etc., quests for self-determination.

World War I Wilsonian minorities' self-determination; post-World War II non-European/racial self-determination; and contemporary ethnic self-determination.

National Self-Determination

One of the difficulties of treating national self-determination is the broad use of the term *nationalism*. Today the term is used instead of the quest for self-determination (defined here as the aspiration to rule one's self, not to be ruled or controlled by others) to denote decolonization (where not nations but colonial legacies were to become independent), the drive for autonomy (which does not necessarily entail independence and full sovereignty), anticommunism (denoting an ideological commitment to the nation-state against internationalism and antinationalism), ethnic awakening (as subnationalism), multiethnic or multinational nationalism (where the ethnic identity of the nation does not exist), and additional instances. The inflation of the term *nationalism* also encourages the inappropriate use of the term *nation-state* for multinational states, and the use of the term *nationalist* as a positive term to denote, for example, the credo of the good citizen, or, the same term, as a negative term to denote an old-time reactionary.

It is possible to argue that in some of these cases the term *nationalism* and its derivatives are appropriate, or at least explicable. However, the term has been so misused that it now confuses terminological clarity. The terms *nation*, *nationalism*, and *national self-determination* may appropriately be used for the German, Italian, and other movements in nineteenth-century Europe and for later movements elsewhere that followed the pattern of unification of diverse entities in the face of a foreign "them." From the late eighteenth century on, the right to self-determination especially stirred Germans and Italians, who had come into intense contact with French people and culture during the upheavals of the Napoleonic Wars. The noted scholar of nationalism, Hans Kohn, writes:

Concepts of the French Revolution spread to Italy and Germany, were eagerly learned from France. But the emphasis shifted: the tyrants to be expelled were French influence and French armies of occupation; the liberty worshipped was *not so much individual freedom from authoritarian government as national freedom from foreign governments.*[9]

The "us" of the people, as opposed to the "them" of the authoritarian ruler changed in the nineteenth century to the "us" of the German and Italian nations opposed to the "them" of the French nation and French foreign rule.

The German word *Volk* probably expresses best what *nation* came to mean. The connotation of the word embraces the German sense of history (*Historismus*) of this *Volk*; it emphasizes national uniqueness and the German people's unifying sense of community. The German "nation" gives the state an indivisible, homogeneous content.[10]

Through their philosophers, poets, and intellectuals, the Germans expressed the wish to free themselves and their culture from French domination, exacerbated by the Napoleonic Wars. The German and Italian "us" unified and enhanced the already existing notions of ar. ideal fatherland. They and other Europeans were pursuing *national* self-determination. An outstanding example is Belgium. In 1830, the Walloon *and* Flemish peoples rose against the alien Dutch rule and then chose to remain members of a single state.[11] In this period of national self-determination, the "them" was not a foreign ruler but the rule of an *alien nation*. Thus, once liberated from Dutch alien rule, the Belgians offered the crown to a royal heir of France and then to a German prince.[12] Russia, France, and Britain went along with the principle of national self-determination when, during the 1820s, they supported the Greeks' rebellion against Ottoman rule. The revolutions of 1848, particularly that of the Magyars in Hungary, struggled against alien Austrian rule. In 1867, Hungary, undisturbed by her own internal ethnic heterogeneity, won an important battle in her quest for *national* self-determination from Austria by obtaining virtual autonomy.

Scholars often use the terms *nation* and *ethnic group* synonymously.[13] It may be correct that a nation is a politicized ethnic group of sorts if ethnic group is defined not as an organic social unit but as a self-defined entity based on the shared language, culture and history that we associate with ethnicity. It may possibly also be correct to say that German national self-determination (or nationalism) created through the process of nationalism a German ethnic group.

I stated above that national self-determination is unifying; we may add that it is integrating and that it is centrifugal. (The words *unifying*, *integrating*, and *centrifugal* are used here interchangeably, for my purpose is to contrast national self-determination and ethnic self-determination.) In these characteristics it differs from disuniting, disintegrating, and centripetal ethnic self-determination and from Wilsonian minorities' self-determination of World War I. Furthermore, national self-determination inspired peoples— Germans, Italians, Greeks—to *create* modern nation-states. Ethnic self-determination, as we shall see below, emerges within the framework of the state that nationalism has often created. It emerges in states where democratic representation, if not adhered to in practice, is at least paid lip service.

National self-determination, or nationalism, then, is a type of self-determination with specific characteristics applicable, par excellence, to the nineteenth-century German and Italian cases. Even today, however, the term is appropriate for movements that unify, integrate, are centrifugal, and emerge among people who do not yet have a state. National self-determination was not confined to the nineteenth century, nor was every quest for self-determination in the nineteenth century national.

In sum, nationalism is a type of quest for self-determination that bridges over religious, ethnic, and linguistic differences and thus functions as a centrifugal force in pursuing its goals. We may also add, without further elaboration, that nationalism needs the state as a machinery to administer problems caused by these differences.

Marxist Class Self-Determination

It would be presumptuous to attempt to discuss this complex issue in full within the framework I have allotted myself here. Not only is reinterpreting Marx an arduous task, but class conflict is not commonly analyzed in the context of self-determination, and thus such a proposal necessitates a separate study. Basically, my argument is this: Marx was originally a Hegelian nationalist; he supported the national liberation of Poland and the Irish struggle for independence. Marx's contribution was, however, his formulation of a new thesis according to which the fundamental dichotomy and conflict are not between the "us" and "them" of nations, but between polar groups inversely related to the means of production. For Marx, the alien rule is the oppression by the owners of the means of production. The proletariat's quest for self-determination is to establish the true community of "us": a communist society.

While Marx acknowledged that the French Revolution had abolished social stratification, he also recognized that stratification had been replaced by class differences based on the possession of money and private property. In his view, by legitimizing and supporting this relationship, the nation-state becomes the institutional expression of man's oppression. Hence, the establishment of a new national state does not provide self-determination; only a stateless communist society can do this.

All elements of the quest for self-determination are present in the Marxian version: the self-identity of a group of people (the proletariat); the alien rulers (the owners of the means of production); and the "message" (Marx's interpretation of the right to self-determination). This type of quest for self-determination was a competitor of national self-determination in the nineteenth century. The competition between class self-determination and national self-determination found expression in the 1848 revolutions as well as in the discussions among Rosa Luxemburg, Otto Bauer, Lenin, and others at the time of World War I. Class self-determination is still present in later types of quests for self-determination, including ethnic self-determination. Suffice it here to repeat that the aim of Marxism is precisely the same as that of any other type of quest for self-determination: to get rid of alien rule (in this case the rule by the owners of the means of production) and to create a community of "us" in pursuit of the right to self-determination. It does not, of course, imply identical *outcomes*, but these are not our concern here.

Wilsonian Self-Determination of Minorities

Wilsonian self-determination conceived an alternative self-identity, that of minorities, which was appropriate in the historical context of the World War I period in Europe. I consider it a distinct manifestation, although Wilson evidently proposed it not so much as an alternative to class identity, and certainly not to national identity, but as an exportable form of democratic ideology to counter the ideology of Marxism-Leninism. Wilson all along wanted to export democracy, but only after the war did he evolve the packaging of self-determination to "penetrate the market" successfully. Wilson's conception of self-determination is not easy to analyze, because none of his writings or speeches contains a comprehensive statement of his ideas on the subject; the references and allusions, mainly during the years 1917 and 1918, are scattered. A specific reference to self-determination as "an imperative principle of action" was made in a speech on February 11, 1919.[14] A less explicit reference to the principle is found earlier in his "Message to Russia" of May 16, 1917, on the occasion of the American mission's visit to Russia:

We are fighting for the liberty, the self government, and the undictated development of all peoples and every feature of the settlement that concludes this war must be conceived and executed for that purpose. . . . But the readjustments after the war must follow a principle and the principle is plain. *No people must be forced under sovereignty under which it does not wish to live.* No territory must change hands except for the purpose of securing those who inhabit it a fair chance of life and liberty.[15]

The famous Fourteen Points, pronounced at a joint session of the Congress on January 8, 1918, do not mention self-determination, but five of the points make more or less specific allusions to it.[16] Article III of Wilson's first draft of the Covenant of the League of Nations contains the term:

The Contracting Powers unite in guaranteeing . . . territorial readjustments . . . as may in the future become necessary by reason of changes in the present social conditions and aspirations or present social and political relationships, pursuant to the principle of self determination.[17]

A host of similar statements support the principle that every people has the right to decide its own fate and destiny. Detailed elaboration of these references to the principle was made by later scholars, but not by Wilson.

A striking aspect of Wilson's concept of self-determination is that it referred to "those nations and territories whose destinies had to be resettled *in one way or another* because they had been unsettled by the war."[18] This remark highlights the primary feature of the Wilsonian notion of self-determination: it was an optional means of settling a limited range of problems at the close of the war. These problems included the future boundaries of Europe, the future of Germany, the threat of Bolshevik influence in Europe, and the maintenance of peace among nations. Wilson suggested the formula of self-determination as a solution to these problems, not as a basic ideology with universal applicability. This does not mean that Wilson's self-determination did not have its roots in a creed or ideology. As Cobban points out, "The key to the understanding of Wilson's conception of self-determination is the fact that for him it was entirely a corollary of democratic theory. His political thinking derived, by way of the American democratic tradition, from the democratic and national ideals of the French and American Revolutions."[19]

The basis of Wilson's self-determination was democracy. He intended to propagate this ideal within the framework of self-determination. The notion of democracy in and of itself did not have sufficient power or appeal in the given historical context, but cloaked in self-determination, that certain people have the right to choose their own destiny, fell on receptive ears among the elites in Eastern Europe because it evoked not merely the democratic principle of individual freedom, but also memories of 1848 and the freedom of nationalities.

When Wilson appealed to "people," he did not mean human beings in general; he meant the underrepresented minorities and, within them, the politically conscious, the elite, who had rocked Europe with nationalist fervor in the mid-nineteenth-century revolutions and who had searched for new outlets for their voices in the beginning of the twentieth century.

Wilsonianism vs. Leninism

Wilsonian self-determination might well have remained one of the obscure formulas for solving Europe's boundary problems and her postwar misery. But the close of World War I found the quest for self-rule in the service of two opposing ideologies: "Wilsonianism" and Leninism.[20] Confronted with the Leninist doctrine of self-determination for nations,[21] Wilsonian self-determination for nationalities became a refinement of the basic World War I concept of fighting for freedom from domination in Europe.

In *Political Origins of the New Diplomacy, 1917–1918*, Arno J. Mayer shows how both the Allies and the Bolsheviks, to promote, respectively, democracy and the world revolution of the oppressed classes (or class self-determination), appealed to patriotic feelings in battered Europe. "As a student of the March Revolution, Trotsky suggested that one of the Provisional Government's chief functions had been 'to short circuit the revolutionary energy of the masses into patriotic wires.' " On the other hand,

the Traditionalists in Paris, London, and Washington who had gradually rediscovered the potency of the nationalist idea, prepared to extend their full backing to the bourgeois-nationalities movements. By the end of 1918 *le Temps* recognized that since communism could not be defeated with "barbed wire" alone it was imperative to oppose it with a rival ideal.[22]

Again, it was not the Marxist-Leninist ideology, developing since the end of the nineteenth century, that prompted Wilson to formulate and press his ideas, but the concrete moves on the Russian side in connection with the ongoing war. Bowing to Soviet pressure, the Russian Provisional Government, on April 9, 1917, issued a statement on self-determination that represented "the first official public pronouncement on the vital issue . . . that the purpose of free Russia was not domination over other peoples . . . but the establishment of a permanent peace on the basis of the self-determination of peoples."[23] Then came the Peace Decree of November 8, 1917, and the Bolshevik six-point program announced at the Brest-Litovsk Peace Conference of December 22, 1917. Mayer writes,

It was through Bolshevik insistence at Brest-Litovsk that self-determination became "a dominant interest" for the diplomacy of the war. For many years Lenin had realized that although Western statesmen and reformers were thinking about the possible and probable application of this principle, they did so within a purely European context. . . . By November 1915 he concluded that it seemed senseless to seek a solution to the problem of self-determination in Europe without also considering the non-European world. Clearly, Lenin struck out in two directions which were foreign to the main body of the Western self-determination doctrine. First, he established the inextricable connection between the national movements and the class struggle; second, he posited the right of national self-determination as a universal principle.[24]

Only by understanding the parallels between Wilsonian and Leninist policies within the contemporary diplomatic context can the message of Wilsonian self-determination be understood. Both notions of self-determination reached out to the people over the heads of their governments;[25] both offered the people the right to self-determination; and both aimed at changing the existing world order. As a Marxist, however, Lenin aimed at class self-determination and the overthrow of bourgeois democracy; Wilson wished to spread bourgeois democracy. Van Alstyne has stated:

It is a remarkable fact—one, I think, of tremendous historical significance—that the concept of the "New Diplomacy" emerged simultaneously from Washington and Petrograd. Although only dimly realized at that time, the U.S.A. and the U.S.S.R. were already rivals in 1918. Wilson and Lenin are the prophets of the new international order. Each in his own way, but in fulfillment of the peculiar mission of his respective nation, struck a mortal blow at the classical system of nation states.[26]

Wilson's self-determination appealed to a sense of patriotism, not to the cultural and historical self-identity of the nationalism of yesteryear. He counted on flag-waving patriotic fervor to realign European peoples and secure a peaceful interrelationship of nations in war-torn Europe.

The influence of Wilsonian self-determination was confined to the European quest for self-rule of his time. What was significant for the future was its strategy of appealing to the people over the heads of their governments to further the principle that people do have the right to self-determination.

Decolonization: The African Quest for Self-Rule[27]

It is difficult to assign the African quest for self-rule to a specific place and period. It is, of course, simplest and correct in a sense to say that the African's quest for freedom began with his oppression, perhaps during the first days of the slave trade. Such a wide approach, however, is too general and analytically useless.

Another difficulty is the existing conceptual confusion of terms: Pan-Africanism, decolonization, nationalism, Negritude; all pertain basically to black liberation. The African quest for self-rule since the French Revolution may be subdivided into two dominant manifestations: Pan-Africanism, formulated in the mid-nineteenth century and persisting as the dominant manifestation until World War II, and decolonization, which began after World War I and continued until the 1960s, the decade of independence. The activation of ethnic identity, in process since the postindependence period, may be considered a third manifestation, but will be dealt with separately. Each manifestation has appeared in several periods.

Pan-Africanism encourages "pigmentational consciousness";[28] it awakens awareness of racial discrimination and aims at personal and social equality within the framework of a given colonial political boundary. To quote Geiss, Pan-Africanism is "an ideology of emancipation from white supremacy"[29] and may be said to have originated in the late nineteenth and early twentieth centuries among blacks in the United States with the evolution of an *African* consciousness. Marcus Garvey professed:

This is the day of racial activity, when each and every group of this great human family must exercise its own initiative and influence in its own protection; therefore, Negroes should be more determined today than they have ever been, because the mighty forces of the world are operating against unorganized groups of peoples who are not ambitious enough to protect their own interests.[30]

In a speech delivered at the Second International Convention of Negroes in New York City in 1921, Garvey said, "We hear among

Negroes the cry of 'Africa for the Africans.' This cry has become a positive, determined one. It is a cry that is raised simultaneously the world over because of the universal oppression that affects the Negro."[31]

Garvey was not alone in protesting. W. E. B. DuBois and Carter G. Woodson figured prominently in the movement, together with individuals like John E. Bruce, cofounder of the Negro Society for Historical Research, who endeavored to instill in peoples of African origin "a pride in their blackness" based on the richness of their African past.[32] Pan-Africanism did not primarily aim at liberation from the colonial framework. As Langley perceptively puts it: "In spite of all this objection to 'alien rule,' there was never any mention of severing relations with the colonial power."[33] Pan-Africanism thus embraces all the movements, protests, conferences, and activities aimed at easing the suffering of the blacks, obtaining more rights for them, and gaining their equality as human beings. The advancement of the Africans as blacks was the dominant feature of Pan-Africanism until World War II.

Decolonization, the second manifestation, and the fourth type of self-determination, was a desire for liberation from colonial rule, a rejection of political domination by a foreign society, especially of a different race, and not merely the will to secure more rights within the colonial framework, as during the Pan-African phase. It ended with political independence from the colonizer. Decolonization began around the time of World War II, and the issues and events of the war had a direct bearing on the institutionalization of decolonization. It must also be said, however, that developments in African society after World War I and the influence of the Pan-African movement had a cumulative effect on the crystallization of aims after World War II. Outside factors included the Atlantic Charter, signed by Churchill and Roosevelt in 1941, which "endorsed the time-honored and time-worn Western principles: a permanent security system, self-determination, and free trade."[34] Also, the Declaration of Liberated Europe section of the 1945 Yalta Agreement stated:

The establishment of order in Europe and the rebuilding of national economic life must be achieved by processes which will enable the liberated peoples to destroy the last vestiges of Nazism and Fascism and to create democratic institutions of their own choice. This was a principle enunciated by the Atlantic Charter—the right of all peoples to choose the form of government under which to live—the restoration of sovereign rights and self-government to those who had been forcibly deprived by aggressor nations.[35]

The Yalta Conference decided to convene a United Nations Conference on April 25, 1945. The United Nations Charter drawn up at this conference restated the right of peoples to self-determination. According to articles 1 and 55, member states must undertake "to develop friendly relations among nations based on respect for the principles of equal rights and self-determination of peoples." Under Article 56, "all members pledge themselves to take joint and separate action in cooperation with the Organization for the achievement of the purposes set forth in Article 55."[36]

The recognition of self-determination as a human right by the international community encouraged decolonization in Africa and Asia both directly and indirectly. Although the right of peoples to self-determination was endorsed far more forcefully than after World War I, none of these ideas was basically new. Since World War I not much had changed except the intensity, the explicitness, and the universalization of the core idea of the right to self-determination.

True, "in earlier centuries the presumption was overwhelmingly in favor of the legitimacy of the establishment and maintenance of a colonial empire. . . . Now the situation has turned sharply in the other direction."[37] One might add that although the "growing conviction among the 'civilized' nations that the old order is no more acceptable"[38] contributed to the success of decolonization, it was not these external factors, together or separately, but internal changes within African society which brought about the shift from Pan-Africanism to decolonization. These internal changes included the faster spread of education of Africans in Africa and abroad, urban growth, and economic changes. Only with the termination of foreign rule could the growth have meaning and the problems that foreign rule had created be solved. Decolonization was the quest for liberation from colonial rule,

prompted by the perception of this rule as the hindrance to the realization of Pan-African aspirations toward basic human equality.
Rupert Emerson wrote:

The breaking point is the universally demonstrated unwillingness of peoples, as they come to an awareness of themselves in the modern world, to
tolerate being run by aliens or to continue subordinate to a foreign state.
. . . The simple truth is that, once a certain state of development is passed,
colonial peoples will not accept good government as a substitute for self
government.[39]

Not until the Second World War did a significant number of African leaders conclude that the only, the inevitable solution to the
suffering, injustice, discrimination, and exploitation of the black
was termination of the political rule of their oppressors.

In this discussion of decolonization two terms are noticeably
absent: nationalism and independence (or independent statehood).
The term *nationalism* has been omitted intentionally, for it is inappropriate for both the Pan-African phase and the decolonization
phase. In neither period did self-identity of a group as a *nation*, in
the proposed sense, dominate; instead, at different times and with
varying intensities, the sense of exploitation, or self-identity of
race, color, and geographic region, dominated. Of crucial importance was that most African states inherited colonial boundaries
drawn practically without regard to ethnic composition.

Independence—or, more exactly, the state—has been ignored
in this discussion not because independence was unimportant, but
because the state was seen only as a tool, a means, ultimately the
only available institutional device to replace colonial rule. Having a
sovereign state is symbolically important and gives the requisite political status in the current world order; however, the goal was not
state creation but expulsion of alien, white rule.

Pan-Africanism and decolonization were phases of the universalization of the right of self-determination. They parallel Wilsonian self-determination, for all three champion freedom from
domination. Beyond this, the influence of Wilsonian principles and
their connection with the two African manifestations are less obvi-

ous. There is evidence that Wilsonian ideas have reached beyond the European and North American continents. The 1920 National Congress of British [West] Africa (NCBWA), convened by J. E. Casely Hayford in Accra, echoed Wilsonian principles.[40] The Indian historian and diplomat K. M. Panikkar writes that in Asia, Wilson's Fourteen Points were acclaimed as a "doctrine of liberation."[41] But it has also been said that "Wilson brushed off a [Japanese] demand for racial equality."[42] However, in Emerson's words, "The promulgation of self-determination as one of the guiding principles of Allied policy came too early in the development of colonial nationalism to have its impact felt to the full immediately."[43]

I have not discussed the decolonization of other peoples because my purpose is not to provide a complete historical account but to outline a type of quest for self-determination: decolonization. By the term *decolonization* I do not refer to an historical period, but to a form of self-determination that has appeared, as have the four other types, at different time periods. By *decolonization* I am referring to the activation of a non-European, a racial identity. Thus, the Indian fight for independence from British rule, Arab awakening against British and French mandatory rule, as well as today's black African fight in South Africa, are, as we shall see later, manifestations of decolonization, the quest for self-determination through the activation of non-European/racial identities. That the whites in South Africa and the British and French in the Middle East have not been formally colonial rulers makes little difference to the people who oppose them. The common factor, I suggest, is the people's perception of Europeans as "them."

The Ethnic Factor

In a 1972 article, Walker Connor complained that the question of ethnic identity tended to be ignored in the literature on integration and nation-building theory, and he listed a sample of ten publications from the years 1960 to 1970.[44] In a 1976 article, however, Pierre L. van den Berghe complained, "Everybody began to talk of the 'revival' of ethnicity. . . . Now everybody (or nearly so) is on an ethnic kick."[45] Both observations, made a mere four years apart, are correct, for Connor's statement refers to the 1960s, van den Berghe's to the 1970s.

How can both complaints be well founded if it is true that ethnic identity is probably as old as humanity itself and the terms *ethnic*, *ethnicity*, and *ethnic group* have been in constant use, at least by anthropologists, for some time? Have political scientists and sociologists, "theoreticians of integration," merely ignored the terms and the phenomenon? Glazer and Moynihan argue that ethnicity "seems to be a new term."[46] Is this really the case?

Although the terms are not new, the widespread activation of an "ethnic identity," with at least implicit separatist demands vis-à-vis the political center of a sovereign, independent, modern (nation-)state, *is* new. This potentially separatist role of ethnic identity was born roughly in the second half of the 1960s. The theorists of the 1960s ignored ethnic identity, for it was a negligible factor in the process of integration and nation building; they may, perhaps, have been shortsighted not to foresee its possible emergence.[47] The "nearly everybody" on "an ethnic kick now" rightly acknowledges ethnic identity's crucial role today.

In the immediate post-World War II period, in Europe and elsewhere, there was genuine acceptance of nation building, unification, and state building. In the newly born states of the non-European world it was probably genuinely believed that the nation-state, imported from the Western world, would promote integration, amalgamation, and unification, just as economic aid would promote development. In the Western world as well in this period, the preoccupation was with physical rebuilding as well as with nation and state building. In the face of the perceived threat from the "East," energies were directed toward strengthening European (nation-)states as viable political entities and as pillars in an economically integrated Europe.

In short, the postwar period saw a process of integration and consolidation of nations and states which scholars faithfully observed, reported, analyzed, and "modeled" through theories of modernization, nation building, and development. In these theories, nation, state, political parties, participation, mobilization, and communication are the central concepts, not ethnicity, which was considered a subject appropriate for the anthropologist. From the end of World War II until the mid 1960s, scholars, including historians and political scientists, were on the *national* "kick" because every political *actor* was on such a "kick."[48]

The dominant role of ethnic identity, or, as it is at times referred to, "disintegration," emerged as the process of "integration" slowed down. Interestingly, this occurred at about the same period in North America, Western Europe, and in the non-Western world—in the mid 1960s. In the United States, civil rights legislation was already on the books, including plans for integration. In Europe, the Marshall Plan had produced wonders: mass poverty was prevented, social mobility proceeded, the Cold War was perceived to be relatively dormant, and former European colonies had become independent. In Africa there was a brief honeymoon of many nationalist leaders with their respective populations until the mid-sixties. In sum, *the new phase began in much of the non-Western world after consolidation of independence and in the Western world after consolidation of economic growth and the perceived lessening of the immediacy of the "Communist threat."*

From the point of view of the state, "disintegrative" forces set in when sections of populations began to perceive that the governments, the political centers, did not or could not respond to the always existing aspirations for material goods and freedoms. Within this newly evolved context (when the economic boom had largely eliminated class distinctions through social mobility in Western Europe and the United States, and class distinctions had not yet been institutionalized in Africa and Asia), sections of populations found themselves in confrontation with their respective political centers, and ethnic identity lent itself as a convenient rallying point for confrontation. Ethnicity has not been reborn, but *the political role of ethnic identity is emerging as an availble aggregating identity by which to challenge the political center*. Ethnic identity, originally an historical phenomenon, assumes a politi-

Emergence of Ethnic Self-Determination, 1960s to 1970s

ETHNIC IDENTITY OR REGION	STATE	ETHNIC IDENTITY OR REGION	STATE
Europe		*Asia*	
Basques	Spain	Pakistan	India
Catalans	Spain	Bangla Desh	Pakistan
Bretons	France	Mollucans	Indonesia
Occitains	France	Muslims (Mindanao)	Philippines
Corsicans	France	Tamils	Sri Lanka
Scots	Great Britain	Nagas	India
Welsh	Great Britain	Kashmir	India
Scotch-Irish (Protestants)	Northern Ireland	Singapore	Malaysia
Manx	Great Britain	Sabah	Malaysia
Jura	Switzerland	Sarawak	Malaysia
Walloons	Belgium	Karens	Burma
Flemings	Belgium	Kachins	Burma
South Tyrol	Italy		
Africa		*Middle East*	
Senegal	Mali Federation	"Muslims"	Lebanon
Biafra	Nigeria	Turks	Cyprus
N. Nigeria	Nigeria	Kurds	Iraq
S. Sudan	Sudan	Armenians	Turkey
Eritrea	Ethiopia		
North & South Angola	Angola	*"Socialist States"*	
Ewe	Togo/Ghana	Croats	Yugoslavia
Huttu	Burundi	Montenegrins	Yugoslavia
Katanga	Congo	Serbs	Yugoslavia
Maores	Comoros	Macedonians	Yugoslavia
Luo	Kenya	Ukrainians	Soviet Union
		Magyars	Rumania
North America			
Quebec	Canada	*Latin America*	
British Columbia	Canada	—	—
Eskimos	Canada		
Puerto Rico	U.S.A.		
Indians	U.S.A.		
Black separatists	U.S.A.		

Source: Various secondary sources, including newspaper reports; not first-hand knowledge of all cases. The list is therefore tentative. Also note that the names listed under "Ethnic identity or region" are often labels or indicators and do not always pinpoint the specific group identity (e.g., "Muslims" in Lebanon). The list is provided for orientation only and to stimulate area specialists to further research, possibly in terms of the thesis presented here. Note the absence of cases in Latin America.

cal role when it becomes the most readily available group identity for the realization of individual aspirations for goods and freedoms.

What is the nature of this phenomenon? The term that has hitherto most forcefully expressed the meaning I attach to this phenomenon is *ethnonationalism*. The term is used by Walker Connor to refer to the "internal discord predicated upon ethnic diversity" in scores of modern multinational states.[49] Among the better publicized cases are those of Biafra, Bangla Desh, the Scots, Quebec, the Basques, and Eritrea.[50] Ethnonationalism, writes Connor, is the exercise of the right to self-determination by an ethnic group, and as such, ethnonationalism has its roots in philosophical notions of the seventeenth and eighteenth centuries that the right to rule is vested in the "people." The French Revolution is viewed by Connor as ethnonationalism's first manifestation; since then, for approximately two hundred years, ethnonationalism has spread throughout Europe and beyond.[51]

The persistent spread of ethnonationalism, argues Connor, challenges the view propounded in theories of modernization and nation building that nation states had an assimilating impact in Europe and would have a similar effect elsewhere.[52] Furthermore, as ethnonationalism is viewed as the exercise of the *right* of self-determination, ethnic groups challenge the legitimacy of existing multinational states. Consequently, ethnonationalism is viewed as a national liberation movement.[53]

I believe the phenomenon of ethnic identity can best be understood by studying its connection with the notion of self-determination.[54] It is not my purpose here to outline the growing literature on ethnicity, nor even the literature focusing on the political context of ethnicity.[55] My aim is only to demonstrate the relationship of ethnicity with self-determination. This connection has already been made in several articles by Walker Connor,[56] and I shall draw on Connor's thesis and expand it.[57]

Ethnic Self-Determination

A premise of Connor's thesis is the redefinition of ethnic identity. He emphasizes that "ethnic consciousness"[58] and "ethnic

imperative"[59] have the potential for radically redrawing today's political map.[60] The deep difference between Connor's meaning and
those of other scholars is, however, implicit. He writes that the
more popular explanations[61] of ethnonationalism (ethnic awakening) by scholars are: the theory of relative deprivation, anomie,
"center-periphery" relationship, and loss of prestige by the political
system and consequent loss of pride by the ethnic group. The fundamental difference between at least the first three explanations of
the other scholars and that of Connor is that relative deprivation,
anomie, and center-periphery relations lend themselves to manipu-
lations by the powers that be; ethnic consciousness stemming from
the separate identity of the ethnic group does not, or at least not
readily, for it is based on an inalienable right. Connor does not believe that ethnonationalism can be contained,[62] while other scholars
do. Connor considers ethnic awakening a right held by the ethnic
group as a "basic human category."[63] This argument deserves
close scrutiny, for whose "rights" are involved?

The most specific definition of "ethnic group" in Connor's
writing is in his article "The Politics of Ethnonationalism," where
he writes, "Ethnic groups have existed throughout recorded history."[64] In a footnote, he explains, "The term 'ethnic group' is
used in this paper in its pristine form,"[65] which derives from
" 'ethnos,' the Greek word for nation in the sense of a distinctive
ethnic group."[66] Ethnic group, according to Connor, is a "basic
human category (*i.e.*, not a sub-group) characterized by unity of
race and culture." Furthermore "it is the acquisition of a sense of
group identity that converts the ethnic group into a nation," or,
probably more precisely (with a rewording of Connor's text), a *national* ethnic group.

Although ethnic group may in some cases be a "basic human
category,"[67] the ethnic group so defined is possibly not the actor
in most "ethnonationalist" cases. The ethnic group, as a basic human category, was certainly not the actor, the awakening group, in
the Biafran secession, in Southern Sudan, in Scotland, in Eritrea,
or in Bangla Desh, and probably not in Quebec.

In the case of Biafra, the Eastern Region of Nigeria, which

sought to become independent Biafra, was composed not of one "ethnic group," the Ibo, but of several: the Ibibio, Efik, Ijaw, and others. Even if we discount the ethnic diversity, because of the questioned loyalty of some of these other groups to Biafra at later stages of the war, the "cultural" oneness of the Ibo may also be questioned. Ibohood is a modern identity. The label was given by outsiders to people speaking related languages in hinterland Eastern Nigeria; the Ibos had neither a common political system nor a common ancestry, real or mythical.[68]

In the case of Bangla Desh, first the *Muslim* Bengalis (together with Pakistan) separated from non-Muslim India; then, as Bengali-speaking Eastern Pakistanis, they seceded from Pakistan. It is doubtful that Bangla Desh can be conceived as a basic human entity, either racial or cultural.[69]

Eritrea is an obvious mixture of ethnic groups, religious groups, and linguistic groups.[70]

To what extent can one speak of a Scottish ethnic identity in the sense of a racial and cultural entity? Are the Highlands and Western Islands, seats of the Gaelic culture, identical racially and culturally with Lowland Scotland? The Shetlanders, for instance, are more Scandinavian than Scottish.[71]

The Southern Sudan had been engaged in a struggle for self-determination for nine years (1963–72) against the Northern Sudan. The common denominator of the Southern Sudanese is their blackness; they are of a large number of ethnic groups clustered into several linguistic groups[72] (and racial groups).

The Basques probably fit Connor's narrow objective definition,[73] as may a few other cases, but certainly not all cases of ethnic self-determination concern the fight by ethnic groups defined in the "pristine form."

Scholars tend to define ethnic group both objectively and subjectively; ethnic realities are there, but they are influenced by situations.[74] I propose, therefore, that under the impact of "situations,"[75] *either* a racially and culturally distinct ethnic group awakens *or* a usually territorially delimited aggregation of human beings awakens and uses—or better, activates—a self-identity—race and/

or language and/or religion and/or common history and/or culture—which outside observers take to be ethnic or associate with the term *ethnic*. Furthermore, the ethnic connotation is strengthened by the existing confrontation between two or more groups, and people tend to accept and then to emphasize the ethnic label because it may enhance the legitimacy of their claim.

Thus, the Basques are a distinct ethnic group; "Biafra" was not. The Biafrans, or Ibos, were a territorially delimited eight million human beings who, in the situation that developed in Nigeria in the first half of the 1960s (and before), became one people. Facing the then Northern Nigerian Muslim Hausa-Fulani people, the Eastern Nigerian Christian Biafrans became distinctly, ethnically, different. The confrontation between observedly different groups helped to create *ethnic* confrontation between the two groups.[76] As one observer put it:

In a short space of time an impressive set of Biafran myths and symbols has been created, and these have been recognized and adhered to by the [Ibo and non-Ibo] population. . . . Even non-Ibo Easterners have given a high degree of support to Biafra. Federal troops occupying Eastern towns have tended to treat Ibo and non-Ibo Easterners alike.[77]

Why, when, or how does a rule come to be seen by human beings as alien *and* opposable? History teaches us that the English were not always *opposed* aliens to the Scots and Welsh, West Pakistan to the Bengalis in East Pakistan, Nigeria to the Ibos, and so on. During decolonization, colonized people in a territory united against the colonizer. I submit that self-determination is in the eye of the beholder; or more precisely, the opposable alienness of the ruler is in the eye of the beholder. An extraterrestrial ruler may face a united "humanity" or "human race."

To repeat the question: Why, then, and how does a rule(r) become "alien" *and* opposable on the basis of the right to self-determination? A possible answer, elaborated upon in chapter 3, would be: The rule, ruler, or rulers become "alien" and opposable on the basis of the right to self-determination when "they" are perceived by human beings as the obstacle to the attainment of personal material and/or abstract goals. I therefore hypothesize that for the Eastern Nigerians, the unitary state of Nigeria became the obstacle to the pursuit of their life as "free people;" English-speaking rule is perceived by French-speaking Quebecois as the cause of a lower standard of living, discrimination in civil service positions, and the like; to Scots, the English are an obstacle, among others, to the utilization of their natural resources for the raising of living standards. In all these cases the "rulers" come to be perceived as obstacles. This perception then prompts the claim to the right to self-determination.

But why did ethnic quests for self-determination appear in the latter part of the 1960s? Once again, Connor's thesis is helpful. First of all, he dismisses the conventional "nation-building" theory that modernization brings about ethnic assimilation.[78] He also argues that modernization did not *cause* ethnonationalism to emerge.[79] Instead he gives three explanations for the emergence of militant ethnic consciousness. First, it is not the amount of contact that causes ethnic awareness, but the perceived threat to the group that the intensity of contact creates.[80] Second, improved communication has carried "the message," recently accepted as a "universal truth," that "any self-differentiating people, simply because it *is* a people, has the right, should it so desire, to rule itself."[81] The third factor is "the evident change in the global environment";[82] for example, today a larger power is unlikely to annex a militarily weak state.

Before we proceed with a critical analysis, an additional point in Connor's thesis should be mentioned. As he and other scholars point out, in group self-awareness, the perceived "others" play a crucial role. To quote Connor:

Ethnic consciousness presupposes an awareness of other groups. The sense of being unique or different requires a referrent, that is, the concept of "us" requires "them." Without the knowledge of the existence of foreigners with alien ways, there is nothing . . . to bind one villager to another. . . . As against members of all other ethnic groups ("them") the two [villages] are united psychologically in the collective "us."[83]

I will attempt in the following to expand Connor's thesis, which I accept in principle. I start with the proposition that it is not only the ethnic group per se, as a "basic human category," active in contemporary ethnic self-determination, that we outsiders, including scholars, associate with ethnicity, but also groups of human beings who define themselves by identities. If we add to this the argument made above that in the time of the French Revolution the individual *human* right to self-determination was proclaimed, and not the *national* (ethnic) right to self-determination, then Connor's thesis might be expanded. The "message" proclaimed in the French Revolution about the right to self-determination fell upon the ears of people who came into intense contact with others and felt threatened by them. This intense contact is occurring now, in the second half of the twentieth century, *within* the framework of the modern sovereign state; the changing global environment facilitates the translation of the message into action. In other words, the message is the same; it is amplified and heeded by people in the modern state. The catalytic impact of modernization[84] was not present prior to World War II to effect ethnic self-determination; it *was* present after the war.

Modernization brought about integration and also spread the message. Then the process of integration slowed down; the message, however, still sounded loud and clear. The quest for self-determination was there, and the glue to unite people was needed. National self-determination does not now make sense, because its embodiment in the (nation-)state is precisely the problem; class self-determination is less available, for one reason because of social mobility; minorities' self-determination is impractical, because the issue is not democratic rights, strictly speaking; racial identity is out, because the rulers cannot be defined in these terms. Ethnic —linguistic, cultural, regional, and historical past identity—lends itself as an effective adhesive, and the ethnic group emerges. This description is greatly simplified to make the point that *the very same people, in different circumstances, could have activated other than ethnic identities.*

Contemporary ethnic self-determination, Walker Connor's

"ethnonationalism," it not a new phase in a centuries-old struggle for recognition by ethnic groups. It is the quest for self-determination by individual human beings who, perceiving the modern state, of which they are members (or perceiving its government) as obstacles and motivated by the idea of self-determination, activate an ethnic identity as a weapon in their quest. Thus, in Europe, folkloric remnants of yesteryears may turn out to be tomorrow's politically active ethnic groups demanding autonomy or independence. West Germany's national unity may turn out to be Germany's ethnic mosaic. It depends not on the existence or number of ethnic groups in Germany but on the perception of Germany's inhabitants and the relative potential of the ethnic identity in comparison to other identities in the eyes of leaders. Africans are not more prone to "tribalism" than Europeans because the African is (still) attached to his "tribe" while the European is not; the African is more prone to "tribalism," to ethnic self-determination, if and when other identities such as class are less available to him. The evidence: twenty years ago the African was "capable" of overcoming his "tribalism" by joining with other "tribesmen" in the fight against colonial rule, activating a non-European/racial identity.

We have to ask, therefore, not whether there are strong ethnic groups or deep cultural and historical heritages, but whether the message has arrived. Does the perception exist? Which identity can be most effectively activated? In Latin America, as in many other parts of the world, the message has not arrived; in Germany, for example, the perception (for good reasons or bad) does not exist; and in most parts of the world now, ethnic identity can be relatively more effectively activated than other identities.

It is a fact that groups are engaged in the quest for self-determination, be they called ethnic groups, subnations, or ethnoregionalists. The Parti Quebecois speaks for the French-speaking group in Quebec; the Scottish Nationalist party speaks in the name of an historically distinct group of people; the Bretons and Basques claim to be culturally distinct from the French and Spanish, respectively. All these groups and scores of others around the world identify and are identifiable on the basis of language and/or common history and/or common culture, which we conveniently label *ethnicity*. Recognizing these facts, scholars have recently begun drawing the profiles of these groups, explaining and justifying—often retrospectively—the grounds for their political awakening.

More significant, however, is that all these groups of human beings perceive themselves as oppressed, discriminated against, or dominated by the central government, or, more precisely, by the modern state of which they are now part. It is important to recognize that ethnic (and not other) groups are now engaged in the quest for self-determination; it is important to realize that these groups probably have a reason, and even a right, to claim self-determination. However, it is *crucial* to recognize that these groups of human beings are engaged in the quest for self-determination *because as individual human beings they feel oppressed, discriminated against, or dominated in the political system of which they are part.*

The ethnic groups are not the cause of the quest for self-determination, but its effect. Ethnic groups play a political role today because human beings have arisen in the quest for self-determination. Peoples from Quebec to the Philippines and beyond organize and fight because they are dissatisfied with the conditions provided by their political systems. Our preoccupation with the ethnic groups only distracts us from studying the factors that prompt them to be politically active ethnic groups.

Karl Marx seems to have made a similar error, for he also pointed to the group (in his case, the proletariat) as the historical actor, although he did realize that the focus ought to be on oppression and exploitation. As a contemporary of the Industrial Revolution, however, he believed that the proletariat, the oppressed *class*, is the bearer of the right to self-determination, hence bearer of the revolution, and that the bearer will always be the class. He was wrong. It must be said in his defense that some fifty years after the French Revolution, prior to two world wars, without information about Africa, Asia, except India, he did not have sufficient perspective to see that not only class identity might be activated and not only in reaction to the oppression by the owners of the means of production. But *we* do have the experience of two hundred years and an almost global perspective, and *we* ought not repeat his error. We have seen minorities rise against the autocratic rulers of empires, Africans and Asians as non-Europeans rise against oppressive colonialism, and we now see ethnic groups rise against rulers in the modern state. In all these cases, oppressor and oppressed have been present, but under different identities.

That the five types of quests for self-determination are related to each other is evidenced by the frequent borrowing of terms from one type of quest for self-determination to another. The condition of ethnic groups is often referred to as "internal colonialism," a term first used by Michael Hechter.[85] Ethnic groups are often referred to as "ethnic minorities." If they are militant, the reference is to "ethnic nationalism" or they are said to be engaged in "class struggle." Furthermore, African and Asian anticolonial struggles have commonly been referred to as "African and Asian nationalisms." *Nationalism* is, of course, the most commonly used term for a wide variety of quests for self-determination. Thus, for example, the African decolonization, Nigerian nationalism, and the Biafran ethnic quest for self-determination are all referred to as nationalism. The interchangeability of terms is significant indication of a common basis for all. This common basis is the dissatisfaction of the "ruled" with the "rulers."

I do not claim to have exhausted the discussion, especially not in the connection with the Marxist doctrine. The debate will undoubtedly continue. But the point I wish to make ought to be clear: the ethnic quest for self-determination is only one type of quest for self-determination. It is caused by the activation of what we call ethnic identity. It compels us to study not ethnic groups, but the reasons that bring human beings to activate one of their many available identities against the political framework of which they are part.

In this overview of the period from the French Revolution to the 1960s, I have tried to emphasize the universalization of the idea of self-determination and the changing character of the self-identity as expressed in politically active groupings. In this period of human history, which continues even today, the cardinal element has not been man's aspiration to find his identity in, or to become part of, a nation, but rather the individual human being's aspiration to control his own life, to realize his or her right to self-determination. To do this, individuals assumed at times a national identity, at other times a class, minority, or racial identity. This assumed identity has been correlated with the perceived identity of the obstacles to aspirations: Napoleon and the France that he represented seemed the obstacle to the Germans, the capitalist owner of private property to the proletariat, the oppressive majority to Eastern European nationalities, and white colonialism to African and Asian peoples. Nation has not been a greater, genuinely unifying factor than class, color of skin, and numerical minority; the (nation-)state has not been a more preponderant political entity than the multinational colony. Unless, of course, everything not a class is considered a nation, and the term *nation-state* is stretched to absurdity.

The past two decades have seen the emergence of a new type of self-determination, what we may call ethnic self-determination. The groups that rise in the quest for self-determination are seen as disintegrating forces, balkanizing forces, emerging for some curious reason in the midst of an assumed unity and oneness. The argument is that ethnic self-determination is just another link, another station, in the human quest for self-determination. It is no more or less "just," understandable, or prompted by circumstances than were national, class, minorities', or racial identities. It is potentially no more or less disruptive, violent, opportunistic than the other groups in the past. Its most formidable enemies are not different from the enemies of the former group formations: the political centers, leaders for whom the existing political entity is there to stay, be they Napoleon, the tsar, the emperor, or the colonizing power. Ethnonationalism revisited appears now with a new face of ethnic self-determination; it is no more the old soldier with strength regained, but a recently born youthful warrior.

3 BACK TO BASICS

The thesis presented in this work is composed of the few interconnected propositions touched upon in the first two chapters. One of
the propositions is that the "self" in the quest for self-determination is to be understood as referring to the individual human
being. A closely related proposition holds that groups of human
beings—nation, ethnic group, tribe, class, and so forth—are to be
viewed not as organic sociopolitical entities, but as the results of
the activation of one or more potential individual identities in reaction to an outside stimulation. Consequently, all types of groups are
temporary entities, fluctuating with the changing stimulation. Still
a third proposition is that quests for self-determination have historically appeared as group quests for self-determination, not individual quests for self-determination, because individual self-determination as an institutionalized sociopolitical entity is inconceivable.
Hence, the formation of the community of "us"—nation, ethnic
group, and so on—as the obvious, but often inadequate, substitute
for the realization of the self-determination of the "I."

In this chapter I propose to show, analytically and not primarily in reference to the historical process itself, the dynamics of the
transfer of individual self-determination from one type of group to
another.

Individual Self-Determination

Humanity is composed today of some four billion human beings. By using the term *human beings* I do not mean to imply that
humanity is divided into so many individualists or into so many
self-conscious creatures, nor do I use the term in a normative sense.
I am referring to the biological entities that inhabit the earth.

Each human being has physical features (height, weight, skin
color, etc.), has a gender, speaks a language, has a personality,
capability, intelligence, a set of religious beliefs, and lives in a
specific geographic location. Of course, some human beings share
one or more characteristics, but each human being has his or her
own distinct characteristics or features.

By definition, human beings are social animals, and as such
must interact with each other. In isolation, individual human beings
will not remain human beings for long but will perish physically
and mentally.

As we are social animals, human aggregations have always
existed, and because of genetics, each human aggregation will
share several physical features. The aggregation of human beings
that exists primarily because we are social animals I propose to
call, for lack of a better term, a *functional aggregation*. This aggregation of human beings exists for the sake of survival. It uses a language for communicating, develops certain patterns of interaction
because the individuals live together, has certain religious rituals,
myths, and histories about the past, and so on, as a result of being
together. I submit that for a functional aggregation language is
"merely" a means of communication; religion is "merely" an explanation of the aggregation's roots and existence; its customs and
culture are "merely" a way of doing things; color of skin is
"merely" an existing fact. In functional aggregations, all these elements fulfill a function for the survival as human beings and are
not, in themselves, conscious self-identities for the members of the
aggregation. A language is spoken because it is a means of communication; what we would call a "culture" emerges out of interactions; none of these elements is used as a symbol of identity by the

members of the group. When asked, "Who are you?" a member of such a group would probably reply, "I am I," without reference to a linguistic, cultural, or religious identity. Individual self-determination is most closely approached in functional aggregations.

Functional aggregations are not only a feature of "primitive" societies; they exist today in the most modern settings. Although in functional aggregations the individual human being is *objectively* subservient to customs, religions, mores, and rulers of his society and usually lives in poor material conditions, *subjectively* he has self-determination. Man is "free" in functional aggregations because he subjectively believes that he can freely use a language, can freely express his opinions, can freely practice his religion, can freely behave according to his customs. Subjectively he does not know, or does not care, that objectively for him there is only one language, one religion, one opinion, one set of customs. Alternatives, even if he knows about them, are irrelevant for him.[1]

When I say that the quest for self-determination is, basically, individual self-determination, I am not positing a goal or making a normative judgment, but observing and interpreting what I believe to be a fact: the most fundamental and necessary human aggregations provide, subjectively, individual (or personal) self-determination. *Individual self-determination, to rule one's self, to control one's own life, is a basic given of the human existence.* The ongoing quest for self-determination is aspiration for a functional aggregation, for a subjective self-determination, or, if one chooses, for subjective freedom.

I said that in a functional aggregation, language, religion, customs, and so forth serve functional purposes. Let us now imagine that a functional aggregation is confronted with another aggregation. The two aggregations may live peacefully next to each other and remain functional aggregations. But if the first functional aggregation perceives the other aggregation either as an obstacle to a source of water that the first group wants to use or to the form of goods that the second group possesses and that the first aggregation aspires to, the two aggregations will go through a transformation to become an "us" vis-à-vis "them." The leader(s) of the first functional aggregation will emphasize the identity of "us" vis-à-vis "them.": mountain people versus valley people, one language speakers versus another language speakers, black versus white. This new type of aggregation I will call *conscious aggregation*. Conscious aggregations are formed when an aspired-to point of reference prompts activation of an identity or identities that emphasize the distinction between "us" and "them," the obstacles to "our" aspirations. A conscious aggregation exists not merely because human beings must interact with each other, as in functional aggregations, but because of the need to generate power against "them" in order to fulfill aspirations, to achieve certain aims.

Human beings in a functional aggregation will "naturally" activate the more fundamental identities, such as language, religion, skin color, common customs, and the like, simply because they are available. Thus, we may have two types of aggregations, one functional, the other conscious, both of which may be characterized as speaking one language or having common customs and physical features; in short, both may be characterized as—ethnic groups. But the difference is crucial. For one aggregation, for instance, language is "merely" a means of communication; for the other it is a symbol of identity. The two "language groups," identified as such by outsiders, are fundamentally different from each other. An individual in the functional aggregation when asked, "Who are you?" replies, "I am I"; the individual in the conscious aggregation will reply, "I am a Flamand."

As I have said, functional aggregations exist today in modern states. Most "ethnic" communities in the United States—Irish, Jewish, Polish—are more often than not functional aggregations. They use their own language, dialect, or accent, religious practices, and customs; they have their means of communication, their own roots, their particular way of interactions, and so forth. Objectively, these human beings in these functional aggregations in modern states are subservient to their own traditions, but subjectively they are free. More than this, the other aggregations around them do not seem to pose obstacles to their aspirations; and *as long as this perception exists*, they remain functional aggregations. I propose that *individualism in the United States is the realization of in-*

dividual self-determination within the framework of functional ag-gregations. The continued existence of ethnic communities in the United States as functional aggregations makes possible the subjective perception of freedom for blue-collar workers, the poor, and, in the past, the blacks. The availability of "ethnic" identities in the various functional aggregations reduces to a minimum the emergence of a class identity. But at the same time, the ready availability of ethnic identities for activation poses an immediate potential for the emergence of conscious aggregations. If aspirations are not fulfilled, if obstacles emerge, the identities are immediately available and flare up. The Black Revolution is the most recent example.

Elsewhere, the Bretons in France, the Welsh in Great Britain, and the Ibos in Nigeria had for a long time been functional aggregations. There too the availability of "ethnic" identity facilitated the activation of such an identity.

I have spoken of the transformation from functional aggregation to conscious aggregation. But let us go one step further. I submit that what one considers a *stable*, *well-functioning* (from our perspective) modern state is either of the two alternatives: either composed of one functional aggregation, or, better, is a functional aggregation, or, as the majority of modern states are, is composed of several functional aggregations. The former is usually referred to as the ideal nation-state, where the state is composed of one nation; the latter is usually referred to as the pluralistic state, composed of more than one nation or ethnic group. In either case, a section of the population of the given state may form or become a conscious aggregation by perceiving "others" in the *same* state as obstacles to their aspirations. Here again, a language, culture, or what we usually call ethnic identity may be activated. But the major point is that human beings may perceive an obstacle *within* the framework of the existing state. Thus, an activated identity of inhabitants of a whole state, for example, Israel, against "them," the Arabs, is analytically identical to the activated identity of part of the inhabitants of a state, such as the Basques versus "them," the Spanish government.

In sum: transformation into a conscious aggregation may occur *within* or *without* the framework of an existing state. In both cases conscious aggregations are prompted by perception of "others," have aspirations to rule themselves, and in each case the potential to generate power is identical.

Let us inquire more deeply into the notion of "obstacle" and the activation of identity. Identity is activated in order to form or reform a conscious aggregation for the purpose of generating power *to establish a functional aggregation*, to preserve self-determination, to acquire or preserve freedom and the "good life." In other words, the identity is activated in pursuit of self-determination.

How can we know which identity will be the activated one? Why is ethnic, not class, identity activated? I believe that the activated identity will be the one that can be demonstrated to both the members of the functional aggregation and to outsiders as being the polar opposite of the (projected) identity of the obstacle to "our" aspirations. The obstacle then is presented as oppressors, exploiters, and so on. The polarity between "us" and "them" is needed to point to the *reason* why "we" are being "oppressed" by "them," to facilitate recruitment, and to justify to outsiders the creation of the new aggregation. The specific identity will be chosen according to availability and effectiveness. In France, for example, "class" identity for the Bretons is more "available" and is seen to be more effective than ethnic identity as long as the Socialist and Communist parties are seen by the Bretons as effectively opposing the "oppressors," the government. If the Socialists and Communists should be in the French government and the Breton perception of their self-determination not improve, or if the Socialists and Communists should fail in elections, the ethnic identity will appear more effective, and Socialist Bretons will become Breton Socialists. In Scotland the reverse is true. For the Scots, the ethnic identity is more available and appears more effective than a class identity. In any case, in the quest for self-determination, not the French, the English, the whites, the English-speakers, the colonizers, the capitalists are opposed, but the *oppression* that they represent. The identity label is merely a symbol, not the actual enemy. Hence "communists" easily become "fascists," blacks become poor, Nigerians become Ibos.

The question whether class or ethnic identity is activated is important because of the ideological implications and the present international context. Class is seen as more extremist, more violent than ethnic identity. This is a misconception. The Biafran War, where ethnic identity was involved, resulted in more people being killed than the October 1917 Bolshevik Revolution, where class identity was present. Violence is a function of the intensity of the perceived "oppression," length of the struggle, and the effectiveness of the recruitment; it is not a function of the character or type of the identity. True, people aggregating around class identity enjoy the support, and may speak in the name of, a well-known ideology that gives them strength and a sense of mission to engage in more violent action. But Marxist class groups are not inherently more violent than ethnic groups. Furthermore, the ethnic group's becoming more violent and extreme does *not* make it a Marxist class group.

Before we proceed, I would like to summarize the above arguments. I am questioning the existence of a basic *group* identity. Each of us is one of some four billion human beings endowed with certain features and, naturally, as social animals, living in functional aggregations where we perceive ourselves to be free. In our quest for self-determination, we form conscious aggregations to fight against perceived limitations or perceived threats to this freedom. We are part of an ethnic group, part of a nation, not because we have a basic ethnic or national identity, but because, and as long as, these aggregations provide us with the hope of obtaining through these groups a sense of self-determination. Scholars have had difficulties in defining the terms *ethnic group* and *nation* because they approach them as organic entities, which they are not.

I ought to emphasize again that the proposition that humanity is *not* organically or "naturally" subdivided into nations, ethnic groups, culture groups, tribes but into so many individuals seeking self-determination does *not* imply negation of the need for social interaction. Man *is* a social animal. Human beings have always interacted with each other, and they have done so "naturally." A common mother tongue, an ancestral grave, and uniform socialization have facilitated interaction among people. These factors have made them an aggregate of human beings, but have not made them into organic groups, ethnic groups, or tribes except in the eyes of the outside observer. Any social scientist, like myself, who has done field research in Africa can attest that often when you ask a rural, uneducated African who he is, the answer is: "I am I. I am from here." Then you discover that all these Africans from "here" speak one language, have an ancestral grave, and so on, and you declare: "Here is a tribe." But this is not necessarily so. Of course they have a common language; they must interact with each other for sex, shelter, and obtaining food, and hence they communicate with each other through a language. How could they escape being labeled a language group except by not talking to each other?

That such an aggregate of people usually does become a group is also not questioned; facing another aggregation they activate one or more of their identities: it may be their language, their geographic location, the shading of their dark skin, and so on. This activation may change or disappear along with the changing perception of the "others."[2]

Individuals *are* social animals, hence "naturally" look for patterns of interactions with other human beings. Rousseau's notions of "community" and "general will" were to provide the framework where *both* human aspirations are fulfilled: to interact with others as social animals and to provide *self*-determination. The problem was not only Rousseau's: "The problem for Plato, as it was to be the problem for Rousseau two thousand years later, was that of discovering the conditions within which the absolute freedom of the individual could be combined with the absolute justice of the State."[3]

The quest for individual self-determination does not contradict, nor is it subordinate to, the fact that we are social animals. To put it in even stronger terms, an individual aspires to absolute freedom; he would like, if it were possible, to set up his own personal kingdom. The notion of self-determination is conceptually connected with a group—which we then call nation, class, and so on—because history provides human beings with "others," with processes of institutionalization of patterns of interactions, and savants to explain and justify them. Human beings do not have to belong to a specific society, to a specific nation, to a specific religious group; but they do have to interact with other human beings, a function that today one's own society, nation, and so on help fulfill. Accidents of history created the existing societies, nations, religions; custom and socialization sanctified them. Exclusive group memberships are not necessary; we can, and some often do, switch from one social group to another, from one national group to another. We know that a child born into a family may be adopted by another family, then by a commune, and so forth. As long as the patterns of interactions needed by the child as a social human being are met, the original family may be replaced. We see these switches in adoptions, migrations, religious conversions, and re-marriages. The quest for individual self-determination implies not isolation of the "self," but aspiration to absolute freedom to inter-act with others. It implies the right to change group membership. It does not deny that we are social animals, but seeks liberation from the present institutionalization of social needs into rigid groupings. Permanent social groupings are here *now* and are *now* convenient patterns to provide the needed interaction; and we are deeply social-ized to believe that only these groups are indispensable. In addition to the highly revered and intensively studied seventeenth-century and eighteenth-century philosophers who offered the social contract thesis, nineteenth-century unifying national self-determination and, not least, the perceived dangers from others to our physical exis-tence, all ingrained in us the commitment to groups.

I repeat, therefore, my original proposition that the quest for a community of "us" is the quest for individual, personal self-de-termination. Or, to put it differently, the "self" is the individual. The search is for community of "us," because the institution-alization of individual self-determination has not even been con-ceptualized, let alone visualized. Furthermore, it is the probable inevitability of the rise of a perceived oppressiveness in *any* com-munity of "us" which pressures individuals to search for a new community of "us."

The archetype of human community today, evolved since the French Revolution, is that of the (nation-)state, which, through the democratically expressed will of its inhabitants, is believed to rec-oncile successfully the impossibility of complete freedom with the servitude to sociopolitical frameworks. Not only the (nation-)state, but other social, political, and economic institutions within the (nation-)state, are "reformed" for free man. The monogamous nuclear family, free enterprise, political parties, voluntary associations, and religious institutions of various denominations are all intended to be the frameworks of free man. These institutions are not seen to be forced upon man. Man has developed a national consciousness, a political consciousness, which legitimizes these institutions for him as free institutions. More than this, Western man believes that the development of these institutions everywhere and the emergence to *these* types of consciousness, *are* the realization of man's freedom; the rising up to this consciousness *is* the exercise of the right to self-determination. I propose that this is not the case; contemporary ethnic quests for self-determination indicate that all these are false assumptions. The (nation-)state provides *a* stage in the quest for self-determination. It would be foolish to believe it the last one.

The Target of Aspirations

In describing the transformation from a functional aggregation into a conscious aggregation, I referred to the emergence of another aggregation that is perceived by the first aggregation as an obstacle either to a source of water or to goods that the second group brought with it. In this section I wish to elaborate on this point.

Two propositions will be forwarded. The first proposition is that it is not the mere existence of the other aggregation that prompts the transformation of a functional aggregation into a conscious aggregation, but the perception of this second aggregation as the obstacle to the realization of the aspirations of the functional aggregation. The second proposition is that the aspiration to self-determination, to control of one's own life, is a composite of several elements that can be grouped into the abstract notions of freedom, happiness, and so forth and also into tangible goods, the "good life." To put it differently, the subjective notion of self-determination is determined by the perceived availability of "freedom" as well as the perceived availability of material goods.

In chapter 1, I stated that precise definitions of *freedom*, the *good life*, and similar terms are not always necessary, because people more often than not refer to what are to them vague notions, and hence the notions ought to be treated as vague terms. The revolutionary who shouts, "Freedom now!" or "Give me liberty or give me death!" or the kind person who greets you with, "Have a happy day!" would have great difficulty in defining "freedom," "liberty," and "happiness," and scholars should not do it for them.

There is an additional point. I also propose that the man who shouts, "Freedom now!" does not merely mean to say "I want *more* freedom than I have now" or "I want more freedom of *speech*"; he means *freedom* and the *good life*. In other words, he does not merely demand a more equitable distribution of scarce resources than the ones presently available to him; he wants to *be* free, he wants to *live well*. The terms are not only vague; they are also infinite, absolute. Man appears to strive for a more just allocation of scarce goods, services, and freedoms because that is what outsiders think he may *reasonably* aim for. Scientists, in order to understand human behavior, should at least weigh the possibility that the aspiration is higher. Man is never satisfied with what he has, not because he always wants more, but because deep inside he wants all. Man does not merely aspire to more than what he has, but to everything—without being able to define what "everything" is.

The implications of these propositions seem to be that we are faced not with an ongoing competition or struggle for a greater share of scarce resources and more freedom within a given political entity, but with an ongoing struggle for abstract notions of complete freedom and the good life which appear to exist "out there." We want not what the Joneses have, but what we imagine human beings anywhere, as far as we know, have, as this is represented by the Joneses. I propose to call these abstract notions of freedom and the good life the *targets of aspirations*.

The targets of aspirations are not within the framework of a political unit, but, at least conceptually, are "out there," and brought to us by radio, television, other means of communication, contact with tourists, and so on. Consequently, the ruled do not judge the ruler or government as good or bad allocators of *available* resources, but as being either the intermediary to *or* the obstacle to the targets of aspirations existing "out there." The targets of aspirations are the products of the *human* genius, not of the political system.

The French Revolution is considered here as the originator of the abstract notion of "freedom," and subsequent movements and declarations, especially by international organizations, further disseminated the notion. The Charter of the United Nations, which calls for self-determination and the end of colonial rule, fulfills such a function. The Industrial Revolution accelerated technological development and promoted the idea that technological achievements are to serve *man*. From the Industrial Revolution on, higher technology and its mass production, coupled with effective advertising, made "goods" part of the target of aspirations, at least in the Western world. Freedoms and rights and the technological progress to provide the "good life" are therefore not seen as the resources of a specific state, but are targets for human beings to aspire to, because they seem due them as human beings.

This proposition has certain implications. First, it is not the perceived difference between groups within the same political entity that prompts the quest for self-determination, but of a group's view that it does not receive a fair share of the target of aspirations. Thus, the Basques, who are better off economically than most Spaniards and have greater freedom today than under Franco's regime, still claim the right to self-determination. It is not the relative condition of the Basques to the Spanish that prompts them to the quest for self-determination, but the Basques' perceived notions of "freedom" and the "good life."

Second, the leaders or rulers or governments are not merely seen as being in charge of the equitable distribution of resources, goods and freedoms, in the political entity, but as intermediaries to the targets of aspirations "out there." The ruler or government is judged a "good" or "bad" intermediary. Thus, an authoritarian ruler from among "us," even a dictator such as President Idi

Amin, may provide a greater sense of freedom than a democratic *foreign* ruler. The former is seen to be closer to self-determination than the latter.

Third, the often mentioned activation of identity, the activation that forms groups, is prompted by the perception of the role and characteristics of the ruler, leadership, or government in its function as an intermediary to the targets of aspirations. Let me take this point further. First of all, when I speak of the targets of aspirations and of human beings relating themselves to these targets, I am speaking of the process of transformation from functional to conscious aggregations. Human beings in functional aggregations do not know of the targets of aspirations, or, if they do know, they do not relate themselves to the targets. Individual human beings in functional aggregations, even if they know of the existence of the targets of aspirations, are unaware that freedom and goods are due *them*.

Once leaders, avant gardes, elites, and the educated create the self-awareness, the relationship to the targets of aspirations exists as well. The individual may try to satisfy his aspiration to the targets by joining a political party or by otherwise getting closer to the rulers or government and thus to the targets of aspirations. Voting, demonstrations, and petitions may be other means. This description does not deviate from the conventional description of a functioning democracy or of a functioning political system in general. But the point is that *we*, imbued by the principle of democracy, hold that this is the best one can and/or ought to do. This position is probably based on the assumption that the issue is the equitable distribution of existing goods and freedoms. If this were the case, all one could do would be to improve the channels of participation. My proposition is that this assumption is incorrect. The aspirations are higher; the targets of aspirations are something like absolute freedom and the good life, to which greater participation is not always seen as a satisfactory answer.

There are, however, a few exceptions. It is true that until quite recently, and for the most part even today, Americans *internalized* the targets of aspirations. All that one could aspire to has been *here*. This was in part because of the economic and

technological achievements of the United States and in part because
of the successful discrediting of foreign ideas that promised higher
degrees of freedom, such as socialism, communism, internationalism, world government, and the like. Not least responsible in discrediting these ideas are the Cold War and those immigrants who
escaped to the United States from the threat or limitations of these
"freedoms" in Czarist Russia, Germany, and other parts of the
world. Because of the internalization of the targets of aspirations,
the aspirations have in fact been lower—evolving around the distribution of what is *available* within the system, not reaching for targets out there. Such a system in the United States allows a democratic give and take, political stability, and the virtual absence of
radical political organizations. It is clear from this that it is not democracy that creates, say, a happy, satisfied society—but a
satisfied society allows the functioning of democracy.

Additional exceptions in the same category are, to a greater
or lesser degree, the socialist states—the Soviet Union, China, East
European states, North Korea, and Vietnam, and possibly "self-
reliance" states such as Tanzania. All these states have attempted
consciously to internalize the targets of aspirations, so far as both
goods and freedoms are concerned. What is "out there" in "the
West," in "the capitalist world," is to be considered irrelevant. To
what degree such states succeed in inculcating these notions is a
separate question. One may add that *because* there are supposed to
be *different sets of targets of aspirations* from the point of view of
the various "camps"—"the peace camp" (East) and "the free
world" (West)—and to the degree that the two sets are a reality,
the reconciliation between the peoples of the "camps" is more
difficult.

Apart from these exceptions, in most political entities, freedom and the good life are not located within the system, although
often the political leadership, as a means of control, discredits the
targets of aspirations "out there" as "alien" ideology and an
"alien" way of life.

When individuals themselves realize or are convinced by others that they do not have a fair share of the target of aspirations,
then the rulers, leaders, government, or simply certain other indi-

viduals are perceived, not as intermediaries, but as obstacles, to the targets of aspirations. From this phase on, the individual human being, together with others who effectively or potentially perceive the same deprivation vis-à-vis the targets of aspirations, will activate the identity that stands in the sharpest contrast to an identity of the obstacles. The sharp contrast, the polarization of the identities of "us" vis-à-vis "them," is needed in order to rationalize the confrontation, facilitate recruitment, and make the confrontation more effective. So the oppressors and the oppressed, the exploiters and the exploited, the racist and the colonized, and other polarizations are born. This description does not negate the fact of exploitation and so on; oppression and exploitation *are* realities. However, not all oppressions and exploitations are viewed as such. The inverse is also true: a perceived polarity of today may not have been viewed as such yesterday. Proletariat versus bourgeoisie, black versus white, French-speaking versus English-speaking (in Canada), Muslim versus Christian, Palestinian versus Israeli, and so on are polarizations created in actual situations. In each of these pairs the first identity has been activated as the opposite of the projected identity of the "other." These polarized confrontations are not givens: proletariat and bourgeoisie, black and white, French-speaking and English-speaking, Muslim and Christian, Palestinian Arab and Israeli individuals have been known to live together, to interact with each other as "us," in various places at various times. At other places or times the sharply contrasting identities are activated.

In figure 1 the dots represent individual human beings, the triangular form the political entity (state), and the dots at the top of the triangular form the political leadership, elite, or government of the given political entity. The stars above the triangular form stand for the targets of aspirations: freedoms and goods.

When the layer at the tip of the triangle—the rulers, leaders, government—is perceived as an obstacle to the achievement of aspirations, self-identities are activated for forming conscious aggregation(s). In the same political entity (triangle), different identities may be activated by different people vis-à-vis different projected identities of the rulers. For example, in Nigeria of the 1960s, in the Southwestern Region, Ibo identity was activated against the

Figure 1. The Activation of Identity

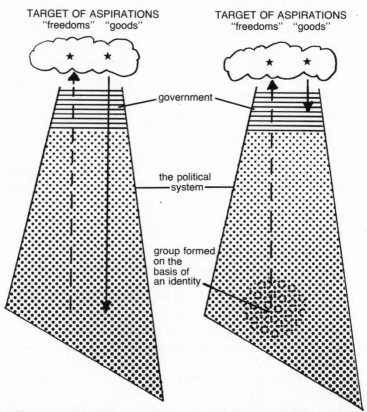

TARGET OF ASPIRATIONS
"freedoms" "goods"

TARGET OF ASPIRATIONS
"freedoms" "goods"

government

the political
system

group formed
on the
basis of
an identity

I. The government is perceived as intermediary to the target of aspirations.

II. The government is perceived as obstacle to the target of aspirations by some.

- - - ▶ aspirations ──────▶ allocation • individual human being "dominating" Northern Hausa; Southeastern Region Yoruba identity versus the Southwestern Ibo in the government; Northern Hausa identity vis-à-vis Southerner identity in the government; and so on. The objective evaluation of outsiders about who "dominated" whom in Nigeria of the 1960s is one thing; the subjective perceptions of populations of Nigeria is another. The Biafran War was fought because of the latter (Chapter 4).

We have arrived full circle back to the conscious aggregation or, in short, to the group. This is the same group that is commonly referred to: the German nation, the Ibo ethnic group, the Hungarian minority, the Russian proletariat. The difference is that here it is proposed that "group identity" exists only when individual identities are activated. As has already been stated, groups do not rise in quest of self-determination—individual human beings do.

A mother tongue, common ancestors, a cataclysmic historical event, or a place where a religious act occurred are more readily available elements to activate a common identity. But the same mother tongue may remain what it is, a means of communication; common ancestors may remain a part of folklore; a cataclysmic historical event may become a memory to sink into oblivion; a place where a religious act occurred may turn into a mere tourist attraction.

We tend to say, "Look, they speak the same language"; "Look, they dress the same"; "Look, they revere the same gods"; they are therefore groups. However, Crawford Young has amply documented in his work how "tribal" identities in urban settings formed and fluctuated in reaction to colonial rule, how these "group identities" are not fixed.[4] We have only carried the argument a step further to say that these are not group identities, but a range of individual identities. It is not questioned that human beings are social animals and hence must, and do, interact with each other. But such interactions do not form organic groups. There is no such thing as a nation; there is a word *nation*, which we attach to groups of people on the basis of more or less clear sets of elements. There is no such thing as an ethnic group; there is the term *ethnic group*, which we attach to aggregates of individuals. Humanity is not subdivided into groups but into a finite number of human beings. The human beings activate one or more of their identities, not in order to form groups, but in order to achieve aims, which we have named targets of aspirations. The historical actor is not the group but the quest; groups do not cause revolutions; the quest, the aspiration does. No phase of self-determination, whether national or other, is to be considered final, for no group is terminal or final. The existing states are the outcomes either of conquests or of various types of quests for self-determination. New and still different types of quests for self-determination may exert pressure toward additional states. This does not mean that states are to be dismantled or declared void; it means that we need analytically to understand the meaning of their existence.

Robert Nisbet writes in his book *The Quest for Community*:

The history of a society can be considered in many aspects. It can be seen in terms of the rise of democracy, the fall of aristocracy, the advance of technology, the recession of religion. It can be conceived, as Tocqueville conceived it, as the work of freedom; or, in Bertrand Russell's terms, as the story of power. There is no limit to the ways of profitably regarding the history of any given society.[5]

My thesis is that the history of a society may be profitably regarded as located at a dynamic point in relation to the quest for individual self-determination. Some blocs of human beings have not been touched by it, such as vast populations in Latin America; most others in other parts of the world have passed through one or more stages. Since the struggle for self-determination is an individual quest, it is an endless process.

In this chapter the basic propositions have been sketched in some detail. Certainly more questions were left open than were answered. It is hoped, however, that this treatment will stimulate the reexamination of what Walter Lippmann once called "conventional wisdom" as it regards the human being and his or her society.

4 FOUR EXAMPLES: THE SCOTS, BIAFRA, THE PALESTINIANS, AND SOUTH AFRICA

In the first two chapters I argued that the quest for self-determination originated in and spread after the period of the French Revolution. Since the French Revolution the quest has appeared in five different forms, each dominant during a different time period and, roughly, in different geographic locations. In chapter 3, I focused on the activation of identities by human beings in their quest for self-determination.

This chapter studies four contemporary cases of quests for self-determination: the Scots, Biafra, the blacks in South Africa, and the Palestinians. The cases have been chosen to clarify further my thesis on the quest for self-determination rather than to illuminate the cases themselves. Here I will try to emphasize, through presentation of the cases, that human beings living in Scotland, the eastern part of Nigeria, South Africa, and a section of the Middle East had been members of *functional aggregations* (had not activated any specific identity in a quest for self-determination) and

71

then, because of changing circumstances, activated different identities. Human beings living in the eastern part of Nigeria first activated a non-European/racial identity vis-à-vis the European colonizers, then briefly switched to activation of a Nigerian national identity vis-à-vis every other state, then again switched to the activation of a Biafran identity vis-à-vis Nigeria. The Palestinians switched in turn from a non-European/racial Arab identity vis-à-vis the Zionists, to a national Palestinian identity vis-à-vis Israel. The South African blacks are now activating a non-European/racial identity vis-à-vis the whites, and, when their present quest is attained, will probably activate ethnic identities vis-à-vis other blacks in a pluralistic South Africa.

By noting the shifts from one identity to another, I want to demonstrate not only that human beings will activate different identities to reach the target of aspirations, but also to show that the five types of quests do not belong exclusively to the periods in which they were dominant. Thus, the Scottish quest for *ethnic* self-determination occurs today, in the latter part of the twentieth century, at the same time as Palestinian *national* self-determination and South African black *non-European/racial* self-determination. Any of the five types of quests for self-determination (and still further new types) may emerge at any future time in any part of the world according to the utility of a particular identity in the quest for self-determination.

In chapter 3, I introduced the concept of the target of aspirations. In this chapter I will show, through the concrete cases, that it is cognizance of the target of aspirations which prompts activation of identity in the quest for self-determination, and not the objective behavior of the "oppressors."

The four cases are presented as illustrations to clarify my thesis and to introduce a method for analyzing what we commonly call "internal conflicts." The method will undoubtedly have to be improved in order to fit the more or less subtle differences among cases. But even in its present primitive form it purports to improve our understanding of the meaning of events that often make the daily headlines.

The Scottish Quest for Self-Determination

Since the union of the parliaments of Scotland and England in 1707, as for centuries prior to that date, the northern part of the British Isles has been a geographic location where human beings, the Scots, had their own religious, educational, and legal institutions. These institutions helped to maintain a distinct accent, a distinct style of life, and memories of a common history.[1] Nevertheless, throughout the years, the Scots have remained, with occasional fluctuations, what I have called a functional aggregation.

Economically, Scotland has been tied to England, and in this sphere Scots have often felt deprived. But this sense of deprivation did not prompt an intensive quest for self-determination. Until the late 1950s, Britain was an imperial power, and many Scots found an outlet for their economic frustrations through colonial service. The Scottish elite sent their children to English public school and prepared them for the then existing opportunities *within the British system* in their efforts to reach the target of aspirations. Although there existed, possibly all along, a general anti-British sentiment among the Scots, it was expressed prior to World War I by many Scots through support of the Liberal party, which in turn supported, at least through slogans, Scottish home rule. Scottish laborers, on the other hand, members of the Scottish Trades Union Congress, considered socialism the appropriate remedy for the economic deprivation of the Scots.[2] In sum, a clear-cut *Scottish* identity as a political weapon was not effectively activated until the 1960s. Why was Scottish identity activated in the 1960s?

The latter part of the 1950s brought important changes. Marshall Plan aid to Great Britain tapered off. Britain did not join the Common Market, and the colonies gradually became independent. The British economy started to decline, which heavily affected the Scots. For example, the colonial service was no longer an outlet for Scottish manpower. At the same time, the expansion of television and other means of communication brought the outside world, the target of aspirations, clearer and closer, including the message that small and poor former colonies were becoming independent. In

the 1960s the British government changed, in the perception of
many Scots, from being the intermediary to their aspirations to becoming an obstacle to them. This prompted activation of the Scottish identity vis-à-vis the *English* government for political aims
through the strengthening of the Scottish National party, in existence since 1928.

Class identity probably was not more successfully activated
because unlike the case in France and Italy, there is no tradition of
strong Socialist and Communist parties in Great Britain to be the
effective aggregators and supporters of a class identity. It is also to
be noted that in 1964 the Labour party returned to power in
London, but the imbalance between England and Scotland—the
Scottish perception of being dominated by the English
government—did not right itself. As Labour did not fulfill the
hopes of many Scots, the SNP appeared as a radical alternative. It
was a radical alternative because the SNP did not represent just another political party, but a program of separation from England on
the basis of a Scottish identity. A respected student of Scottish politics, James Kellas, writes: "The poor performance of Britain in
world affairs, the decline of the British Empire, and the new-found
status of small countries in the U.N. may have contributed to the
feeling that Scotland could reasonably 'go it alone.' "[3]

It is often stated that the rise of "Scottish nationalism" was
caused by the discovery of the oil in the North Sea off the shores of
Scotland. I question this view. Kellas's authoritative book was
written before the discovery of oil in 1973. In Kellas's account of
"Scottish nationalism," offshore oil does not play a role in the political success of the SNP from the late 1960s until 1970. It is an incorrect but generally held view that oil gave birth to a genuine
Scottish drive for separation from England, but the perception of
deprivation and hence the aggregation around an ethnic identity
started before the oil crisis and persisted not solely because of the
prospects for economic wealth. The SNP considered that as an independent state Scotland could "go it alone" not because of the oil
but because other small countries can.

With all this said, it is also unquestionable that the discovery
of North Sea oil in 1973—considered by the SNP as belonging to a

future independent Scotland—was a momentous event and politically advantageous for the party. For four decades the SNP scarcely drew votes and had no representatives in the British Parliament. Then, in the two 1974 elections, the SNP polled 21.9 percent and 30.4 percent of the votes cast. (*See* table 2) But party growth was considerable prior to the discovery of oil. In the 1959 elections, the SNP collected only 0.8 percent of the votes in Scotland; in 1964, prior to the oil discovery, 2.4 percent, almost three times as many. The jump from 1964 to 1966 is again more than twofold. Similar jumps occurred from 1966 to 1970 and again in 1974. The leap from a single member of Parliament in the pre-oil-discovery elections of 1970 to seven in the February 1974 elections and then to eleven MPs by October 1974 is impressive; but to go from one to eleven MPs is not an eleven times but less than three times growth of electoral support in seven years. This rate of growth was not unprecedented in the pre-oil-discovery years.

In answer to the question: "Why did Scottish nationalism begin to make political waves only in the 1970s and not twenty,

Table 2.   General Election Voting in Scotland, 1929–74

ELECTION YEAR	CONSERVATIVE (%)	LABOUR (%)	LIBERAL (%)	SNP (%)	OTHERS (%)	PERCENTAGE VOTING
1929	35.6	41.5	18.2	0.1	4.6	73.3
1931	48.6	32.0	14.1	1.0	4.3	77.4
1935	41.6	36.7	14.1	1.3	6.3	72.2
1945	36.3	47.4	9.1	1.2	6.0	68.7
1950	44.8	46.2	6.6	0.4	2.0	80.9
1955	50.1	46.7	1.9	0.5	0.8	75.1
1959	47.3	46.7	4.1	0.8	1.2	78.1
1964	40.6	48.7	7.6	2.4	0.7	77.6
1966	37.7	49.9	6.8	5.0	0.7	75.9
1970	38.0	44.5	5.5	11.4	0.6	73.4
Feb. 1974	32.9	36.6	7.9	21.9	0.6	78.8
Oct. 1974	24.7	36.3	8.3	30.4	0.3	75.0

Source: *Scotland's Future*, SNP Manifesto, February 1976; see also Milton J. Esman, ed., *Ethnic Conflict in the Western World* (Ithaca, N.Y.: Cornell University Press, 1977), p. 251.

Table 3.   British Parliament Seats Won in General Elections,
Scotland, 1929–74

ELECTION YEAR	CONSERVATIVE	LABOUR	LIBERAL	SNP	OTHERS
1929	22	36	14	—	2
1931	50	7	—	—	17
1935	37	24	3	—	10
1945	25	40	—	—	9
1950	26	37	2	—	6
1951	29	35	1	—	6
1955	30	34	1	—	6
1959	25	38	1	—	7
1964	24	43	4	—	—
1966	20	46	5	—	—
1970	23	44	3	1	—
Feb. 1974	21	40	3	7	—
Oct. 1974	16	41	3	11	—

Source: *Scotland's Future*, SNP Manifesto, February 1976; see also Milton J. Esman, ed., *Ethnic Conflict in the Western World* (Ithaca, N.Y.: Cornell University Press, 1977), p. 251.

fifty, or one hundred years earlier?'' Milton Esman perceptively remarks: "No single factor, not even North Sea oil, can explain a complex development of this scope and scale.''[4]

The growing support for the SNP does not, of course, mean unanimous or even majority support. But our purpose here is not to demonstrate the strength of the SNP as a party but to study the quest for self-determination as manifested in support of the SNP *and* in other ways. The SNP symbolizes the most extreme intensity of this quest—separation; but both the Liberals and Labour have catered to similar aspirations on lower levels of intensity. The Liberal party has long supported home rule for Scotland and federation for Great Britain; the Labour party, and even the Conservatives, have favored devolution of powers in one form or another. Some 80 percent of the voters in Scotland say in opinion polls that they favor some form of devolution,[5] and they may perceive Labour and Liberal party programs as subscribing to the Scottish right to self-determination. The question is then: Will the Scottish quest for self-determination be satisfied by a measure of devolution of powers to Scotland without separation?

We may try to elaborate on this issue by referring to the two terms used in British politics in this context: "devolution" and what is referred to as "Scottish (as well as Welsh) nationalism." In this context, the first term, *devolution*, is to be the answer to the second, *nationalism*. In other words, the intention of the supporters of devolution seems to be to devolve authority to regional assemblies, to Scottish (and Welsh) parliaments, in order to satisfy the "nationalist" aspirations.

In my view the logic is faulty, for devolution of power as planned has very little, if anything, to do with "nationalist" demands. The devolution plan of the British government assumes, overtly or not, diversity of interests in the United Kingdom, viewed as a pluralist entity. Devolution is the granting of greater rights to diversified interests, be they political, economic, or social, in an ethnically pluralist entity. However, what are referred to by the English as "nationalist" demands are in my view a high-intensity ethnic quest for self-determination in which two ethnically self-defined groups (if we include the Welsh as well) confront the state of which they are part. Devolution is proposed as a governmental and administrative reform; it proposes to reform the "system of *government*." This type of reform is possible, to follow our model, so long as the political leadership is perceived as an intermediary to the aspired-to goals. When the leadership is perceived as an obstacle, when a group of people perceives itself to be discriminated against, a reform of the political leadership is of little help. As an analogy we may recall that Africans and Asians in their fight for terminating colonial rule would not accept reformed colonial government in lieu of independence.

The Scottish National Party (SNP) has been relatively successful in persuading a section of the Scottish voters that the *British* Parliament, devolved or not, cannot be an intermediary to their aspirations. They say, in fact, that no form of devolution except the fulfillment of aspirations will reduce the intensity of the quest for self-determination. More than this, devolution, if implemented, is seen by the SNP as a stepping stone to a higher intensity of activity toward independence.[6]

The difference between devolution and "nationalist" demands is understood by a Labour MP from Scotland who opposes, first of all, the SNP. He writes: "Devolution is concerned with democracy, and is not itself an answer to the problems of the economic and social malaise affecting parts of Scotland."[7] He supports devolution, however, since it is not an instrument of separation.

Let us now turn to another question. Is the Scottish quest for self-determination analogous to a nationalistic, cultural fervor, as nineteenth-century German nationalism was? Esman correctly observes:

Scottish national identity has meaning primarily in reference to the English "they." It is weak in positive cultural content and in cultural grievances. Despite the efforts of an earlier generation of literary and romantic nationalists, and despite the continuing concern of some SNP activists, the great majority of modern Scotsmen do not define their deprivations in cultural terms and cannot be mobilized emotionally or politically against the English on language or cultural issues. This is true of all classes, regions, and age groups.[8]

The issues are rather economic grievances than emotional, nationalistic devotion, says Esman, which in part explains the absence of violence.

It seems to me that the lack of emphasis on a cultural identity is because Scotland has always been recognized as a separate entity and has been a functional aggregation, having her own legal, educational, and religious institutions; hence the affirmation of her separateness is not needed. In the eyes of the Scots and of the English, Scotland exists as a separate entity. What the SNP advocates is recognizing this fact and granting independence.

Furthermore, violence is not a derivative of a commitment to a cultural feature, but of the intensity of the quest for self-determination. Now that the Devolution Bill has been defeated, we must await the actions of the British government to see whether the Scottish quest for self-determination will or will not switch to an even higher intensity and, hence, possibly to violence.

The Scots as a territorially delimited group of human beings were of course not born during the last decades; they have existed for centuries. Neither was the relationship with England, which may be characterized at times as confrontation, a new phenomenon. But the economic and political difficulties of the British government, including Britain's decline as an imperial colonial power, greatly increased the perception of the British government as an obstacle to the aspirations of Scots, which prompted the emphasis of a Scottish group identity, a conscious aggregation, as a political weapon vis-à-vis an English political center. This identity has been activated by the SNP, which aims at independence for Scotland.[9]

To summarize: It is not the discovery of oil that prompted the Scottish quest for ethnic self-determination; the current relatively militant stance of ethnic self-determination is not a linear continuation of past demands, but a new one; and the present rivalry against the English is based on neither language nor religious issues, but is a political confrontation between human beings who now rather identify themselves as Scots than Labour or working class or a language group. Economic difficulties do not necessarily effect class self-awareness; perceived economic hardship—relative deprivation—will promote the most effective group identity to confront "them."

The Case of Biafra

Two hundred years ago the enormous region where Nigeria is located today was sparsely inhabited by some 10 to 20 million human beings. Some of them had lived in the region for centuries as functional aggregations; others immigrated at various periods from other parts of the African continent and possibly from beyond.[10] Naturally, these peoples brought with them and later developed different customs, used different languages, had their own sets of ancestors to be worshiped, their own religious practices and patterns of interactions with each other. Furthermore, as they settled in different geographic regions, their sources of livelihood, styles of life, and behavior toward their neighbors differed. For example, the Muslim Fulani people subdued and mixed with the Muslin Hausa people and settled in the arid regions of today's Northern Nigeria, where the absence of the tsetse fly permitted the use of horses. The northern people, a century ago, had virtually no contact with their later cocitizens in the southern tropical regions.

Colonization was imposed by foreigners—white Europeans—on these peoples. This imposition involved the regulation of the Africans' political, economic, social, and cultural lives by law and by physical force. It resulted in categorization, classification, unification and separation, building and destruction; in short, it resulted in pressures for change in directions desired by the colonizers. It also activated ethnic identities vis-à-vis the colonial government. To facilitate the perpetuation of the foreign, British rule, the colonizers created a territorially delimited Nigeria, with three and later four internal regions. Each of the regions had its own elections and government, in addition to the federal parliament and later government in which all participated on the basis of proportional representation. As the Muslim North had approximately 50 percent of Nigeria's population, it had a larger share both in the colonial federal parliament and the Lagos government, which alienated the peoples of other regions, who generally regarded the Northerners as backward traditionalists. This is important for understanding ensuing events.

Elections held in Nigeria under colonial rule in 1959 had been relatively orderly, but after independence, when the issue became who would control the government—the intermediary to aspirations—first the 1964 Federal and then the 1965 Western State regional elections were marred by corruption, violence, and disorder.

The North, as well as the East and Midwest, threatened secession in the midst of the 1964 elections, rather than tolerate "others" in the government and being dominated by "them." Controlling the federal government was not a question of having or not having political influence, but of either ruling or not ruling oneself. Furthermore, the enormity of the crises and countless acts of political violence, involving kidnapping and bloodshed, showed the seriousness with which the stakes were perceived. Repeated references to the Nigerian electorate's ignorance of the "rules of the game" are undoubtedly well founded. In Nigeria, and elsewhere where democratic elections are held, victory in elections is viewed not just as a mandate for exerting political influence, but as a license for political domination. The "game," then, is not a competition to secure greater opportunities for political power, but to gain political domination over the losers. The crucial difference between old democracies and newly independent states such as Nigeria is that in the former, the parameters, the extent and meaning of domination, have already been set, or at least supposedly so; in a newly independent state they are not, or usually not. For example, in the United States the voters trust that neither a victorious Republican nor Democratic administration will nationalize private industry, ban newspapers owned by sympathizers of the rival party, appoint relatives to key government positions, or violate in any serious way the principles of the American democracy. Such restraints in the United States were set not by Western civilization per se, but by experience and a Constitution that has traditionally been respected. In the United States the people *trust* that the government dominated by either of the two parties will try to be good allocators of available goods and freedoms for all Americans. In a newly independent state, parameters of government behavior are not set, and the behavior of a future government is not known. Just the opposite: on the basis of experience in their own and in other African states, sections of populations fear that "others" in the government would probably not be intermediaries for all. This expected behavior is set not by African civilization, but by the Africans' past experiences under colonial rule and/or simple lack of assurance.

It is not surprising, then, that the Nigerian elections of 1964 failed, and that the regional leaders had to "fix" the results behind closed doors. The resulting compromise did not settle anything politically, as later events demonstrated, and it did not, as it could not, reflect the true results of the elections. But the continued premiership of the Northerner Sir Abubakar Tafawa Balewa minimized Northern fears of Southern domination, the most critical element in the whole crisis. The compromise was said to have preserved "national unity." This is, of course, a way of saying that the Nigerian state did not fall apart. But national unity could not be preserved, because Nigeria in 1964 had not be nationally united.

Then came the two coups of January and July 1966, which

threatened the unity of the state. Each was entirely different in character.[11] Robin Luckham, in his meticulously researched book on the Nigerian military, analyzes both coups from every feasible aspect and argues that the January 15, 1966, coup was a well-planned military coup against the civilian regime, not the result of the activation of a "civilian" identity vis-à-vis a civilian regime.

During the years after Independence many army officers came to share the growing disilusion with the ruling political class which is common among bureaucratic and intellectual elites in Nigeria. Members of that political class were riven with bitter internal conflict about the division of material and political resources between the regions and the ruling groups that controlled them. They were venal and did not hesitate to use coercion to maintain themselves in office.[12]

This was a military coup with the political intent of doing away with the corrupt civilian leaders. Later accusations that this was an Ibo coup against the North and that it led to the countercoup of July 1966 do not hold water.

The relevant coup for my thesis is the second, the counter-coup of July 1966. In this coup the military officers *were* the executors of the sentiment of a segment of the population; in this coup there *was* a sense of relative deprivation or a danger that it would occur; in this coup the rulers, the government, *were* perceived as representing an ethnic group; in this coup there *was* an expression of the highest intensity of ethnic self-determination—an attempt at secession. I am not referring here to the secessionist attempt of Biafra, which came later, but to an attempt at secession by the North, for this coup was carried out by Northerners with a sense of relative deprivation against a political center dominated by Ibos.

The turning point was Decree No. 34 of May 1966, issued by the military government headed by the Ibo Major General Ironsi, which "purported to do away with Nigeria's federal constitutional structure and make the country a unitary state. The decree confirmed the Northerners' fears that the military regime aimed at depriving them of power and a separate identity."[13]

The plans to do away with the federal system demonstrate the importance of a changing relationship to the political center. As

long as the Hausa-Fulani in the North, the Ibo in the East, and the
Yoruba in the West had their own regions, they could feel a sense
of autonomy, of self-determination, through their regional governments. Once they faced the one political center directly, their sense
of deprivation became stronger. In a short time after the second
coup, the issue was not only Biafra's secessionist threat, but the
"dismantling of Nigeria."[14] In May 1966 riots in the North cost
the lives of many Ibos residing there. From then on, mutual hostili-
ties and suspicions grew, and plans for the July 1966 coup were
made.

The July coup was successful, in the sense that the Northerners, under Lieutenant Colonel Gowon, took over power in Lagos,
after the murder of Major General Ironsi and many others. It is important to note, however, that the initial intention of the Northern
officers was to secede from Nigeria. "The main spokesman for
this view was Lieutenant Colonel Muritala Mohammed, and he and
other like-minded officers started to make arrangements for the immediate withdrawal of all Northern troops and civil servants in
Lagos back to their region."[15] Unlike the January 1966 coup, the
aim was not to take over power in Nigeria, but to separate from
Nigeria. The leaders were persuaded not to do so on condition that
Gowon, as the most senior Northerner in the Army, should take
power. Gowon agreed, but he could not secure the consent of the
military governor of the East,[16] Lieutenant Colonel Ojukwu, the
later Biafran secessionist leader. Ojukwu's proposal was either that
Agundipe (a Yoruba), the most senior Nigerian officer after Ironsi,
be head or that the Northerners' original proposal to split Nigeria be
accepted.[17] Gowon refused.

Only then did the third and most publicized phase of events,
the Biafran secession, begin. It did not come out of the blue sky.
First of all, the Declaration of Biafra's Independence did not come
until May 1967, after several months of abortive negotiations. Second, as we stated above, secession was treated as an acceptable optional solution to the Nigerian situation, even by many who later
opposed and fought the Biafran secession. In the aftermath of the
July 1966 coup, secession was one of the options considered along
with federation and confederation. Secession later was abandoned

as an alternative when civilian leaders, civil servants, and others
with an interest in maintaining one Nigeria prevailed. Even then,
when Ojukwu finally decided to secede, it took all Gowon's skills
to persuade other regions not to follow suit but to join in the effort
to keep Biafra in.

Another factor that spurred Biafra's secession was the further
massacre of Ibos, during September and October 1966. This time
many thousands of Ibos were killed or mutilated, and some one
million Ibo refugees left their Northern homes for the Eastern Region. This massacre not only exacerbated Ibo feelings toward the
North, but also fueled the ensuing conflict.

There is an additional point to clarify. As in the case of the
Scots, oil is mentioned as a reason for Biafra's secession attempt.
Such an explanation is unfounded. To quote from Luckham,

> It would be overstretching even a Marxist interpretation of history to say
> that oil was the root cause of the civil war. But given that the basic lines of
> cleavage were political, with their source in ethnic and regional conflict
> and in the figure of the army, oil and the foreign earnings it produced were
> among the *essential means of struggle*.[18]

We have noted earlier that the separatist option was considered not
only by the East, but first by the North, which does not have oil.
The separatist option simply was in the air in Nigeria throughout
1966 as *a* solution to the political situation. It was considered as a
structural alternative to avoid subordination to another region.

The oil existed in non-Ibo areas of the East on the Atlantic
Coast, within the Eastern Region under the administrative jurisdic-
tion of the military governor of the East, Lieutenant Colonel
Ojukwu. True, Ojukwu refused to negotiate the creation of new
states in the oil-producing sections of the East, for access to both
the oil and the sea was strategically important. Neither was the oil
crucially important for the Federal Government, at least in the initial stages of negotiations with the East. To quote again from
Luckham's study:

> Taking into account the rapidly increasing output of the Midwest [Region],
> oil in the Eastern minority areas was certainly not the major portion of the

total *Federal* production; nor did oil yet provide a very high percentage either of Nigeria's foreign earnings or of its governmental revenues, even though it was rapidly growing.[19]

As in the case of the Scots, oil may have been factor, but it certainly was not the reason for the East's perception of the nature of the Nigerian federal political center.

The Western parliamentary system had been imported into Nigeria, as elsewhere in sub-Saharan Africa, from the outside. Before independence it was believed that the Nigerian political center would be the intermediary to the aspired goals of development and modernization. These expectations failed; the political center turned out to be an obstacle.

But who were the obstacles? In Nigeria, probably more than in Britain, the political center could more readily be perceived on an ethnic basis. The creation of political parties exacerbated the ethnic basis of politics; also, the federal regional system had been commonly, though not officially, identified with the three major ethnic groups. The size of the Northern Region's population meant the proportionally large representation of the Hausa-Fulani, with all the negative connotations of this for the people in other regions.

There has not been in Nigeria an alternative to the ethnic perception of the political center. "Class lines in Nigeria are quite fluid," writes van den Berghe,[20] and in no way competitive with ethnic identity. To say that in the early 1960s Nigeria was ruled by the right or by the upper classes may be objectively and statistically true, but it was the subjective perceptions that brought about the July 1966 mutiny and the Eastern secession. In July 1966, the Northern officers did not revolt against a capitalist class, but against what they perceived to be Ibo domination; during the months of 1966 and early 1967, Ojukwu did not negotiate with a class-dominated central government, but with what he perceived to be a Northern-dominated government. In May 1967 he declared independence for Biafra, not from a capitalist state, but from a political entity in which he perceived the Ibos would be subordinated.

The Biafra secession failed, but Ojukwu's worst fears were unfounded. After two and a half years of fighting, the Federal troops and government proved magnanimous victors. The creation of first twelve and then seven more new states was a political recognition of the ethnic identities that form the Nigerian federation and has been a workable arrangement under the rule of the military.

The Palestinian Identity

The Palestinian case demonstrates well the difference between outsiders' definition of a group of people and that group's self-identity.[21] We often hear the questions: Why suddenly Palestinians? Who are the Palestinians? They have always said that they are Arabs; they used to say that they were part of the "Arab nation." There are some twenty-one Arab states. Why can't they join any of these, as Arabs?[22]

These questions may be answered analytically thus: the Palestinian identity and the notion of Palestinian nation were created by the activation of an identity deemed more effective in the eyes of Arab refugees and other Arab inhabitants of the geographic region of Palestine in their quest for self-determination. For thousands of years there had been no Palestinian identity or "nation"; as in the case of other peoples, the identity and the nation have been created as a weapon.

The geographic area that much later came to be called the Middle East has been inhabited by human beings, later classified as Semitic peoples, living in numerous functional aggregations. Some of these peoples, who may have differed from the others in various respects, became the Jewish people; the others came to be known as Arabs because—and probably only because—they spoke a language called Arabic. To put it differently, from the point of view of objective identity (chapter 3), an Arab is one who speaks the Arabic language and whose ancestors came from a geographic region called Arabia. Subjective Arab identity was not born until the late nineteenth century, and then only on a limited scale. Until that time, and to a great extent even today, if one asks an Arab "Who are you?" the answer is likely to be "I am I" or "I am from this *watan*," meaning roughly "home, place, or setting."

At first the Arab identity was activated to create Arab nationalism vis-à-vis the Turks, the Ottoman Empire; later it was directed and strengthened vis-à-vis the cultural, economic, and political influence of the European West. As in the case of the Africans and the Asians, the dichotomy was between European and non-European identity in all of its manifestations. One of the manifestations of the European identity, influence, or threat was perceived to be Zionism, first of all because most Jews came to the geographic area of Palestine from Europe, and second because they set up "colonies," or settlements, with some financial help and moral support from the colonial centers of the time: France and Britain. Zionism was perceived as part of the colonial scheme, I would suggest, not because it was felt to be part of European colonization, as it was not, but because the settlers, the "intruders," and their supporters were of European origin. The European identity of Zionism was needed, then and later, successfully to activate a non-European (in this case Arab) identity.[23]

In 1948 the modern state of Israel was born. It continued to be opposed as a Zionist colonial entity in the 1948 war of independence and later. However, in the 1956 and 1967 wars, and in military clashes in between, Israel did not fight with Arabs as such (for they did not all participate), but with particular states. The Arabs versus Zionism confrontation, the non-European/racial identity versus European identity, weakened and gave place to activation of Egyptian national, Syrian national, Jordanian national and Palestinian national opposition to Israeli nationalism, the Israeli state, as well as to each other. The 1956 war gave a push to the activation of a Palestinian identity, and the 1967 war strengthened it even further. Let us recall that after the 1956 war the United States and after the 1967 war France, seemed to side with the Arabs. Hence, these two wars could no longer be effectively presented to the Arab masses as wars against European/white colonialism. One ought to add to this the interest of the Arab states in enlisting the Arab refugees—only later self-identified as Palestinians—to be in the front line of the fight for an "Arab cause." Thus, a Palestinian national identity was activated against Israeli nationalism, and Israel was opposed as the obstacle to the realization of their particular aspirations for national self-determination. This Palestinian national

self-determination lost to an extent the strength that an all-Arab
identity provides, but gained strength by activating and uniting refugees, formerly feuding traditional clans in the West Bank and
Gaza Strip, Palestinians living in exile, and so on, thus largely
bridging the regional, clan, religious, and class differences among
Palestinians.[24]

A Palestinian identity was actually created. Objectively
viewed, Palestinians do not have a separate history, a different language, or a separate culture from other Arabs; they are also
Muslims and Christians, as are other Arabs. For years after 1948
they had been Arab refugees, Arab minorities in Israel; they were
so referred to by the Arabs themselves. It is not the Palestinians
who have awakened in a nationalist fervor; a functional aggregation
of Arabs have awakened and have activated a distinct, separate, potentially more effective Palestinian identity. They created a new
conscious aggregation, a people called Palestinians, who are now
creating their separate history, culture, and institutions.

It is one of the arguments of my thesis that human groups are
not "natural" entities, and the Palestinians exemplify this. In the
past there had been no Palestinians as such. They are not an out-
growth of a separate culture or separate early history. They were
born through the activation of an identity vis-à-vis the Israelis. The
Palestinians are not unique. If Jews had not settled in Israel in the
twentieth century, there would be no Israeli identity or Israeli nation today, in spite of the fact that Jewish states did exist in the
same location some two thousand years ago, and in spite of the fact
that a separate Hebrew language did exist. The spoken Hebrew language was revived as the language of Israel, and Jewish history became also Israeli history. Similarly, it can be said about the United
States that the American culture, American history, even an American language have been created by individuals gathered in America
from various countries in the last two hundred years or so. This
feature does not make Americans less of a people than another people, such as the French, who have had an independent state since
A.D. 800.

Palestinians are now a conscious aggregation in quest of self-
determination. If and when Palestinian self-determination is real-

ized in a state, the now bridged over clan differences of various towns in the West Bank and Gaza, the differences between Christians and Muslims (as in Lebanon), and so on may be the bases for the emergence of additional identities against the rulers in an independent Palestinian state, who may come to be, or will be viewed as, predominantly representing one of the clans, one of the towns, one of the religions.

In the Palestinian case we can clearly see three types of quests for self-determination: Arab, (that is, non-European/racial) against Zionist "colonial" rule, Palestinian national self-determination against Israeli national self-determination, and possibly ethnic self-determination against the rulers of their own government or state in the future.

From the point of view of those who identify themselves as Palestinians, twenty-one Arab states cannot solve the problem of the Palestinians, because none of them is a Palestinian state. A Palestinian identity is now born; this self-identity vis-à-vis Arabs is similar to the self-identity of a Nigerian vis-à-vis other Africans. Whether it is sufficient reason to establish a Palestinian state or to have a different outlet, such as autonomy, for their quest for self-determination is not our concern here. The point is that they now perceive themselves as not "merely" Arabs but as Palestinian Arabs, just as Nigerians today are not merely blacks or Africans, but Nigerian blacks or Nigerian Africans.

South Africa

While the South African case is sensitive, it too can be analyzed in terms of the quest for self-determination. In spite of flagrant racial segregation and oppression, South Africa is inhabited by 25 million or so human beings. By this I mean to say that for purposes of analysis of the South African situation, one ought not begin by pointing out the four- or five-part racial divisions: Europeans (or Afrikaners and English-speaking whites separately), blacks, coloreds, and Asians. In the present political climate, of course, the racial division is most salient, but not all inhabitants of South Africa have always acted upon these identities in the past,

not all of them do in the present, and probably not all of them will
always so act in the future. It is convenient, but simply wrong, to
take races in South Africa as organic entities. The English-speaking
whites and the Afrikaner whites, though racially identical, have not
always considered themselves as an "us"; neither have all blacks
so perceived themselves. Nor has there been in South Africa a constant struggle of the blacks for self-determination since the first
day the whites set foot on the continent, in spite of the fact that *objectively* the blacks have always been subordinated to the whites.
There has been constant ad hoc opposition by blacks to various *actions* of the whites, but intermittently most inhabitants of South
Africa have lived for years in what I have called functional aggregations, that is, the blacks long acquiesced in their subordinate position. For years the whites, as the government, have been seen by
a majority of blacks as the intermediaries, and not as the obstacles
to, the target of aspirations, to the extent that these aspirations existed. The most one can say is that in the last few hundred years
there have been attempts at activation of at times a class, at times a
racial identity vis-à-vis the capitalist exploiters or white rulers.

Today the situation is different. The blacks are now in quest
of their self-determination through the activation of a non-Euro-
pean/racial identity vis-à-vis the whites, who are viewed as colonizers.[25] The South African blacks too, as did the Arabs and Africans
and Asians in the earlier process of decolonization, now bridge
over their own ethnic differences. They are all now relatively successfully united as blacks against the whites, who are perceived,
rightly or wrongly, as colonizers.

The successful and intensive activation of the non-European/
racial identity came relatively late in South Africa. It came in force
only in the latter part of the 1960s, while in other parts of the continent and the world it had appeared long before. One may speculate
that there are several interconnected reasons for the delay. First, it
was more difficult to pinpoint the South African whites as colonizers than to so identify the French, the British, and Belgians elsewhere on the continent, because formally, legally, they were not.
Second, and as a consequence, for South African black leaders the
activation of a class identity vis-à-vis the exploiting class of the

whites was for a long time more available than the black pigmentational identity against the whites as colonizers.[26] Thus, while Communist parties had been generally unsuccessful in formally colonized Africa prior to decolonization, the Communist party was quite successful in South Africa, among blacks as well as whites, as early as the 1930s.[27] Consequently, the white South African government confronted the opposition to its rule and battled and banned Black organizations as Communist organizations. The white government still presents the black African quest for self- determination as Communist inspired.

Furthermore, the white South African government built its apartheid policies on the basis of differences among black groups (tribes, ethnic groups) and believed that apartheid was the appropriate policy to separate and rule the various African groups indefinitely. But by delaying the establishment of "independent" homelands, they minimized the possible activation of Zulu, Xhosa, and other identities. Had the Transkei and the other "homelands" been established fifteen years ago instead of now, there possibly would have been a fight for *complete sovereign independence in each of the homelands separately*. Today the homeland "solution" is doomed to failure, mainly because a *black* identity has already been activated and receives widespread support in the outside world. In other words, the activation of a black identity vis-à-vis the whites is today in South Africa the most efficient weapon in the fight for self-determination.

I have previously stated that the choice of the identity to be activated depends on its effectiveness in recruiting followers and generating support for the group's fight for self-determination. What is the relationship between the followers' strength of commitment and the amount and quality of support from outsiders? To what extent does the international support of the blacks' cause in South Africa supplement the commitment of South African blacks to their own cause? Conversely, what would be the faith of the South African blacks in their quest for self-determination without outside moral support, particularly without the support they receive in the forums of the United Nations? One may argue that outside support is crucial.

Whatever the correct answers to these questions, South African blacks do receive widespread outside moral support for their cause, in addition to tangible support, such as military supplies. It is interesting to note that different outsiders do not unequivocally support identical group identities: the United States supports the black majorities without franchise in the name of democracy; the Soviet Union supports an exploited black *proletariat*; and African states support *colonized* blacks. The three types of support coalesce because, as my argument states, all these outsiders support the blacks' quest for self-determination. The United States votes in the United Nations on issues of South Africa against an undemocratic regime that does not allow the majority political participation; the Soviet Union votes against the capitalist-imperialist ruling class; and the blacks vote against the white colonizers. The *effect* of these votes is support for *a* quest for self-determination. The type of self-determination is determined by the South African blacks' view of themselves as blacks oppressed by whites, which allows for various interpretations in the forum of the United Nations.

While the United Nations, with its anticolonial stance, facilitates a consensus of support for the South African blacks, the same stance is not helpful in finding a solution to their quest. For if the whites in South Africa are colonizers, the same as whites have been in other parts of the continent, then decolonization means the physical departure of the whites. But, South African whites did not arrive on the continent some seventy years before the projected time of decolonization as did the French, the British, and the Belgians (though not the Portuguese), *and* the South African whites do not have a European mother country as did the French, the British, the Belgians, *and* the Portuguese.

There is of course now the general but quite vague consensus that South Africa ought to become a democratic society in which each individual is an equal political participant. Without even touching on the political complications (for example: how does the Soviet Union define such a democracy?), such a solution, analytically, cannot be but temporary, because in South Africa today *none* of the groups would find the *self-determination* they aspire to in a pluralistic South Africa. The target of aspirations, for whites and blacks, is much higher than the one that the limitations of a participatory democracy would allow. Democracy is the exercise of compromise, and human beings in quest of self-determination are not *willing* to compromise. In the same way as Nigerians and Ghanaians would not share power with whites in the aftermath of decolonization, so blacks in South Africa would not share power with whites after their decolonization. Nor, for that matter, would some blacks be willing to be "colonized again" by other blacks. Briefly, a pluralistic South Africa would lend itself to ethnic quests for self-determination, or to military or foreign takeover to prevent such new quests.

I would risk saying that the solution in South Africa would be to proceed *directly* to an arrangement stemming from an ethnic quest for self-determination. That would mean self-determination for each of the ethnic groups: Afrikaners, English-speaking whites, Xhosa, Zulu, and so on. Practically: this would mean self-government for each group on a more or less delimited territory while dividing the wealth of the country proportionally according to the size of each group. This would be sociopolitical self-determination in an economically integrated South Africa, a framework explained in some detail in chapter 5.

Briefly then, in South Africa as elsewhere, where human beings are engaged in the quest for self-determination it is not the objective situation that motivates them, but their perceptions. Who confronts whom is also not a question of objective racial or cultural divisions, but of activated identities. We are at the stage of decolonization in South Africa not because the whites are objectively definable as colonizers, as the British, French, and others were in other parts of the continent, but because there is now an activation of a non-European identity in the quest for self- determination, the same as elsewhere on the continent some fifteen years ago. The aim of the quest is now decolonization, not because it makes economic sense or because it is an ultimate solution, but because it is aspired to by a people whose quest of self- determination today receives almost universal support.

I have no doubt, as I state above, that a decolonized South Africa, one in which there is one man-one vote, black and white, will not be immune from the activation of additional identities, be they Zulu, Afrikaner, colored, proletarian, or others. Decolonization is the next step because people are *not* driven by the aspiration for democracy nor for majority rule nor for political independence, but by the aspiration to control their own lives and not to be controlled by "others," who presently are the whites. However, the "own" and "others," as I have tried to show, are not permanent, but fluid identities. As the quest for self-determination will not end with decolonization, I have suggested sidestepping it and moving directly toward ethnic self-determination, which might last longer. Without such a move, the quest for self-determination in South Africa will, in my view, inevitably be long, bloody and arduous.

Again, I urge the reader not to view the above analyses as a substitute for a comprehensive study of each of the four cases, but as a further clarification of my thesis. It is important for me that the interpretation and approach I propose be considered and then improved upon, rather than that my expertise in regard to the four cases be evaluated. Let me repeat therefore a few points which the analysis of the four cases is intended to underline.

To the questions "Who am I?" or "Who are you?" the appropriate answer ought to be: "It depends." As any individual in changing social encounters changes his identity from, say, that of teacher to man or to father, by emphasizing one identity over the others, so the individual in political encounters changes his or her identity by emphasizing one identity over the others. The ascendance of one identity over the others may be long-lasting but not permanent. Families, ethnic groups, nations exist in two spheres: in the consciousness of individual human beings and in the official registers and statistics recording the moment. A conscious aggregation of Palestinians exists because a certain number of human beings have activated, or emphasized, an identity separate from others, although in official registers they may still appear as Arabs. Any human group exists through the activation of an identity, sometimes followed by legitimization of the group. To understand social conflict and change, I urge that, for purposes of analysis, registers and statistics be temporarily disregarded.

I suggest that identities are activated when there is a perception, a cognition, of oppression, subordination, exploitation, or domination by "others." This was the perception of people in Scotland, people in the Eastern region of Nigeria, the Palestinian Arabs in the Middle East, and blacks in South Africa. Perception of oppression, real or imagined, does not prompt only Communist revolutions, but a potentially revolutionary movement for self-determination of any type. It is a false assumption to say that ethnic groups mature and become nations. Ethnic groups are born and arise because of a perception of oppression; if there were no perception of oppression, real or imagined, there would be no ethnic self-determination, no class self-determination, no black self-determination, and so on. Conflict, I have already suggested, is a function of perceived oppression, not a function of group cohesiveness, historical consciousness, or cultural exclusivity.

Polarization of identities *is* influenced by objective conditions. The Scots cannot create a black versus white polarity; where social mobility has raised income levels and standards of living, a class polarity will be more difficult to create; in a state with a long history of religious rivalries, such as India, religious polarization will be more available.

In Europe, for example, the specific political history ought to be taken into account: the traditional perception of the "rulers" (especially in France and in Italy) as representing a class, a deeper doctrinaire conviction of intellectuals in the validity of the class conflict, and the existence of a relatively effective institutionalized framework of left-wing parties all successfully counterbalance perceptions of the rulers on an ethnic basis. However, the possible participation of Communists in the governmental process in Italy and the consequent blurring of their class identity, and a similar development in France, would, in my view, hasten the shift toward the activation of ethnic identities among the Bretons, Occitains, and Alsatians in France, and in various regions of Italy, such as Sicily and Sardinia. Demonstrated ineffectiveness of these left-wing parties in the eyes of the "oppressed" would bring similar results. The point is that no one identity, not even the color of skin, is a more "natural," more effective, more permanent unifying factor than any other. The identity does not bring about the quest; the quest creates an identity.

The quest for ethnic self-determination has already made considerable headway around the world. Most cases, however, are said to exist because of local situations and specific conditions under titles of ethnic conflict, subnationalism, and regionalism and are usually *mild* conflicts, unlike secessionist movements, which are viewed as militant. The Scottish movement is often explained in terms of economic difficulties necessitating economic reforms; the Breton movement is often relegated to being folkloric, requiring more tolerance from others; the Eritrean separatists are often explained by foreign subversion and thus acquire global importance, and so on. According to my thesis, the Scots, the Welsh, the Bretons, the Occitains, the Walloons may be viewed as located toward the less militant end of the spectrum of the quest for self determination. The greater their frustrated aspirations to goods and freedoms, the farther they may move toward the more militant end on the continuum, where separatist (secessionist) movements are located.

The potential of ethnic discontent to disrupt existing societies successfully is often downplayed. A noted scholar of the phenomenon, Aristide Zolberg, stated recently:

In the same way most of the societies which were already in the process of establishing a liberal regime before the industrial revolution became the arenas of class conflict that did not lead to revolution, many among them are becoming the arenas of the conflict of cultural communities which do not lead to separatism.[28]

Possibly so. But there appears to be at least one fundamental difference between class conflict and "cultural community conflict" which may influence the prospects of a revolutionary outcome. "Communal revolution," in other words, militant ethnic self-determination, has a greater chance of receiving moral support from a variety of sources than class revolution ever had or could hope for, primarily because it has a greater chance of gaining acceptance on the basis of human rights, even from international bodies. The obvious cases are those of South Africa and the Palestinians. It is not that international organizations and our thinking have advanced to support ethnic quests for self-determination under the banner of human rights; this support in any case has been more verbal than real. The point is that as commitment to the principle of human rights spreads, it will likely be seen as applicable to ethnic groups, possibly as "minorities," "subnations," or "nations." As I have stated, class may be defined as a group of people self-identified on the basis of their relation to the means of production; a communal/ethnic group defines itself on the basis of common language, culture, common history. A communal/ethnic group may claim to be, and may be as seen as, a "people" whose right to self-determination is legally recognizable; a class group cannot claim to be such or be so seen.

This does not imply that overt general support is likely to be forthcoming in the very near future. But it does mean that as the quest for ethnic self-determination spreads and gains strength, there might be a greater inclination to use the instrument of, say, referendum, rather than the weapon of counterinsurgency.

In our description I have alluded to the several types of activated identity: non-European, class, national, and ethnic. In the cases of the Palestinians and the black South Africans I foresaw the possibility of the activation of identities after their present quest for self-determination has been achieved. At the present time, the nation-state is viewed as the entity to which all people aspire. I propose that the quest for self-determination is not motivated by the aspiration for a nation-state, but is prompted by a perceived obstacle to the achievement of aspirations. A future "national" government may also turn out to be an obstacle, which may activate additional identities within the independent state.

This view appears to be contradicted by the situation in Asia and Africa. In these parts of the world, modern (nation-)states have been established during the last two decades or so, but very few separatist movements have emerged. This is usually taken as proof that the quest for self-determination there has largely been terminated. I believe that the small number of separatist movements may be temporary. In many African and some Asian states the political center is still headed by the original national leader, "national" because he at least symbolically united the inhabitants against the colonizers and led the country to independence. These leaders (for example, Felix Houphouet-Boigny in the Ivory Coast, Sir Seretse Kama in Botswana, H.K. Banda in Malawi, Ngarta Tombalbaye in Chad, Leopold Sedhar Senghor in Senegal, Kenneth Kaunda in Zambia, Julius Nyerere in Tanzania, and Sekou Toure in Guinea) are the "founding fathers" of the new states. Such a person symbolizes the political entity and neutralizes the activation of particular identities by his charisma, skill, and the credit he has earned by his achievements. Prospective political leaders who wish to compete for political power are unable to create an effective opposing group identity.

Once these founding fathers depart, however, the opportunities for the competing political leaders will open up to activate existing identities—linguistic, religious, class, regional, tribal, and so on—vis-à-vis the new leader or government. Whoever claims the leadership will not have the aura of respect that his predecessor had. Unless the new political center, including the political leaders, is perceived by *all* sections of the population as an intermediary to the existing target of aspirations, the perception of the new leader as obstacle is likely to be exploited by the opposition. As aspirations are infinite and undefinable, and self-determination is for the individual self, some form of social and political ferment is constant and to be expected.

5 IMPLICATIONS FOR THE MODERN STATE AND THE INTERNATIONAL SYSTEM

The quest for self-determination has hitherto contributed to the birth of nations, the freeing of minorities, the success of the Bolshevik revolution, and the liberation of colonized peoples. In its latest phase, it has been acting as a disintegrative force within the framework of the modern (nation-)state system. In the previous chapters I have touched upon the five manifestations of this quest. My purpose in this chapter is to assess the probable future impact of the ethnic quest for self-determination on societies, states, and the international system.

I should repeat the observation already made that unlike other quests, the ethnic quest for self-determination appears in, and is viewed by, the modern (nation-)state as a disintegrative force. National self-determination united human beings into wider national entities. Minorities' self-determination claimed autonomy and self-government within the framework of existing states (in spite of the contrary example of the breakup of the Austro-Hungarian Empire). Class self-determination has aimed at changing regimes, and decolonization meant the departure of colonial rulers. In the ethnic quest for self-determination, however, ethnic identity is usually claimed by human beings living in a distinct territorial entity;

99

hence, their quest poses the threat of disintegration of the modern state.

The view that we should expect a process of disintegration appears, of course, to contradict the widely held views that the present (nation-)state system is too strong to lend itself to change, and that we should expect, and plan for, integration of states into wider and wider frameworks, possibly on a worldwide scale. To some extent, these views are correct: the present state system appears strong and, if the European Community is considered an example of integration, then integration is also underway. At the same time, however, we are *also* in the midst of disintegration. Since the Second World War, the idea of wider integration has been earnestly pursued, but the complete integration of modern (nation-)states has not been achieved. Now, because of the activation of the ethnic identity, a disintegrative process has set in which may result in entities that do tend toward wide integration. To put it differently: ethnic self-determination results in a kind of disintegration that permits a kind of wider integration toward a new world order. I foresee therefore a fundamental structural change in the international system.[1]

For the purposes of our presentation let us first identify the three ongoing trends: integration, disintegration, and status quo.

The disintegrative ethnic quest for self-determination, together with other phenomena mentioned below, constitute what will be called here the "centripetal trend." Coincident with this trend are the efforts of governments in practically every sovereign state to maintain or achieve national integration or unity, or at least to preserve the territorial integrity of existing states. One may include here elections, administrative reforms, cooptation of ethnic/regional leaders into government, and repression in order to maintain a well-functioning pluralist state, to mobilize political participation on a large scale, or, at times, to suppress dissent. This second phenomenon will be labeled the "status quo." The third contemporary phenomenon is often referred to as "supranational integration," and the most outstanding, and probably the only correct example is the European Community (E.E.C.). This phenomenon, which here includes international and regional organizations and ties as well as supranational organizations, will be named here the "centrifugal trend."[2] The proposition may be summarized in the following four points:

1. Theoretically, wider integration might be possible because the centripetal and the centrifugal trends complement each other, for the centripetal trend gravitates toward sociopolitical entities and the centrifugal trend gravitates toward economic-normative entities.[3]

2. Practically, integration might be possible because both the centripetal and the centrifugal trends are gaining strength vis-à-vis the status quo.

3. The two complementary trends, the centripetal and the centrifugal, also tend to reinforce each other: the greater the economic-normative integration propelled by the centrifugal trend, the greater the possibility (and maybe even the pressure) toward sociopolitical disintegration propelled by the centripetal trend; the greater the sociopolitical disintegration, the greater the pressures (and maybe also the possibility of shift) toward economic-normative integration.

4. The interplay of the two complementary trends is generating an evolving new system, an alternative to the sovereign (nation-)state and the international order: the centrifugal trend has the potential of adapting the economic or productive and the normative functions into wide regional or global frameworks; the centripetal trend has the potential of adapting the allocative and social functons into small communal frameworks; both of these are now at least conceptually vested in the sovereign state. Consequently, the world is not evolving either toward a balkanized world of hundreds of sovereign states nor toward a global society under world government. Because of the split in the absolute sovereignty now vested in the modern state, a sociopolitically disintegrated and an economically and normatively integrated world appears to be emerging.

Yet a fifth and somewhat separate argument is that citizens in search of solutions to even ad hoc problems they encounter in their respective states—social injustice, deteriorating ecological conditions, or political repression—may prompt not only regime change *within* the state (say from civilian to military rule) or ideological change within the given state (say from capitalism to socialism), but also, or instead, prompt a structural change *of* the state, such as secession, change from unitary to federal system, and the like. Consequently, a structural change of a state is the functional equivalent (or a useful concomitant) of a regime (or an ideological) change in a state.[4]

It is convenient to start the presentation with a three-column table, each column for a trend, and each trend with a tentative list of pressures that feed that particular trend. Each "pressure" is identified by a phrase. The table is followed by a brief discussion of each of the four arguments presented above.[5]

ARGUMENT 1:   *The centrifugal and centripetal trends are complementary.*

The centrifugal trend originates in the worldwide confrontation with growing economic problems, in the recognition of the need for large economic frameworks to tackle these problems, in the awareness of a shrinking world and a growing sense of solidarity and interdependence among its inhabitants. The centripetal trend originates in the desire of sections of populations to live in small social units,[6] at least in part as a reaction to the perceived threat of the "mass society" and the burden of "state machinery," as well as in the spreading conscious aspiration for "freedom" and political self-determination. The two seemingly incongruous trends, the centrifugal and the centripetal, moving toward the larger and the smaller at the same time, are complementary, because each trend addresses itself to problems posed by two of the four subsystems of any system: the social and the political on the one hand and the economic and the normative on the other hand. (I am alluding here to the Parsonian theory, which will be referred to later.)

Admittedly, there is no clear-cut evidence to prove that the centrifugal trend is exclusively or even predominantly economic-normative and that the centripetal trend is similarly sociopolitical, as I say they are. I maintain, however, that at least the following functioning institutions are outgrowths of the centrifugal trend: the European Community, GATT, the Organization of American States, the Entente in French-speaking West Africa; so also are universal norms such as "We all inhabit the same planet," and the no-

Table 4. Structural Change in the International System

	COLUMN 1	COLUMN 2	COLUMN 3
Trend	status quo	centrifugal	centripetal
Description	maintaining or aiming at national/political integration	economic and normative integration	sociopolitical disintegration
Sources of Pressure Accentuating the Trend	political authority political power recognition by other governments aspects of international law (territorial integrity, non-intervention) support of citizens Cold War (threat) inertia social scientists, historians	awareness of scarcity of resources third world pressure for multilateral aid and assistance governments' interest in economic cooperation awareness of and respect for foreign cultures Marxist "internationalism" bureaucrats in international organizations academic literature on the future	ethnic quest for self-determination "communalism" "small is beautiful" view "withering away" ideology extreme-left terrorism human rights

Note: The items on the lists are tentative, incomplete, and not ranked in order of importance.

tion of interdependence. Similarly, Quebec separatism, Scottish nationalism, and communes grew out of the centripetal trend. However, to arrive at a consensus on the classification of these phenomena into the two trends is not without difficulties. The major difficulty may stem from the fact that leaders, institutions, and movements themselves do not separate between economic-normative and sociopolitical aspects: the Parti Quebecois appears to aim at complete separation from Canada; the European Community is aiming at full European integration; communes do not aim at being economically dependent. Nevertheless, my contention is that centrifugal trends lead to economic and normative institutions, and centripetal trends lead to sociopolitical institutions. What data can be marshalled to support my contention?

On the centrifugal side, the best example is the European Community. It was born to achieve economic integration, which led to dreams of political unity, but the latter has remained in the category of dreams in spite of the prospects that direct elections to the European parliament seem to hold. Europe is tending toward economic integration, because it is realizable; Europe is not tending toward sociopolitical integration, because it is unrealizable. The elements needed for sociopolitical integration—primarily, the will —simply do not seem to exist in the partner states. It is instructive to quote from a 1967 article by Ernst B. Haas, in which he revised the views he had expressed in his now classic *The Uniting of Europe*, published in 1958:

Not a cultural unity, but economic advantage proved to be an acceptable shared goal among the Six. . . . Each of the Six, for individual national reasons, and *not* because of a clear common purpose, found it possible and desirable to embark on the road of economic integration using supranational institutions. Converging practical goals provided the leaven out of which the bread of European unity was baked. . . . Converging economic goals, embedded in the bureaucratic, pluralistic and industrial life of modern Europe provided the crucial impetus. The economic technician, the planner, the innovating industrialist and the trade unionist advanced the movement, not the politician, the scholar, the poet or the writer.[7]

It would be fruitless to engage further in the debate on the nature of European integration efforts. It is probably instructive, however, to observe that there is not a single international organization that even vaguely achieves world government, or political integration (certainly not the United Nations), while international organizations dealing with economic matters abound: the EEC, IMF, World Bank, possibly OPEC, and the Nordic Council. Beyond that, most of the "pressures" under the column of centrifugal tendency are economic in nature, which may be considered evidence if there is consensus on the composition of the list in table 1.

On the normative side, communication technology, dwindling resources, and decolonization promoted the notion that the "shrunken world" is inhabited by interdependent human beings. The wider perspective on mother earth, the growing recognition of coresponsibility for human survival, and acceptance of the heterogeneity of human beings as one human species are the composites of an emerging universal norm. This universal norm does not, however, imply nor lead to a global sociopolitical system under a world government, as is often predicted. It probably implies and leads to a greater commitment to organizations guided in their work by these norms: UNESCO, UNRWA, organizations dealing with famine relief, Amnesty International, and the like.

Let us turn to the centripetal trend. The fundamental question in the political sphere is the nature of "minority nationalism," or, to phrase it differently, What do people who aim at autonomy or secession *really* aspire to? By what are they really motivated?

The quest for self-determination is not the aspiration to a state, or for the control of economic resources, or for more favorable economic conditions, but an aspiration to control one's own life, to be master of one's own destiny, not to be ruled or controlled by others, but to be politically independent. People in quest of self-determination do fight for full sovereign statehood, which includes control of economic resources, but only because the state is presently the only available institutional framework in which the quest for self-determination can be institutionalized.

Decolonization may be viewed as a phase in the centripetal trend. Colonized peoples' aim was liberation from colonial rule and full sovereignty; they disregarded the economic benefits of continued colonial rule and the economic disadvantages of cutting colonial ties. In most cases, the result of decolonization was political independence and economic dependence on the former mother country. We may recall that in Africa since the 1960s the progressive solution for the undesired form of economic dependence, neocolonialism, has always been "centrifugal" African unity, or economic *inter*dependence.[8]

While in the 1960s economic ties of the new states with the former mother country were an unplanned result of their struggle for self-determination, for people engaged in the ethnic quest for self-determination in the 1970s, continuing ties with the former mother country—Canada, Great Britain, and so on—are also implied. The difference is that the new economic ties are to be based on interdependence. The slogan of the Parti Quebecois is "sovereignty and association," sovereignty for the culturally, linguistically separate Quebec people *and* continued economic association with Canada. The Scottish Nationalist party (SNP) also has declared its willingness to cooperate closely with England and Wales economically—after the separation of Scotland. An independent Scotland would have a near example: the relationship between the Republic of Ireland and Great Britain. Anthony Birch shows in a recent article that while Ireland is politically independent, in economic matters it is closely linked with Great Britain.[9]

The two trends, the centrifugal and the centripetal, are complementary also on the social and normative levels. The very same person who supports the idea of communes favors the slogan "Small is beautiful" and opposes the big "state machinery" is at the same time a proponent of worldwide human solidarity, internationalism, worldwide ecological planning, and so forth. For further clarification let us turn now to the second argument.

ARGUMENT 2:   *The two complementary trends impinge on the status quo.*

The centrifugal and centripetal forces are not only complementary, but are both gaining in relative strength vis-à-vis the "status quo." Not only is there a quantitative, two-to-one confrontation (centrifugal and centripetal versus status quo), the first undermining the status quo from within and the second from without, but also—and more important for the future—the pressures of the centrifugal and centripetal trends are, in the main, gaining strength, those supporting the status quo remain by and large static. As illustrations I will list and briefly evaluate some of the sources of pressure in each of table 4's three columns. To indicate the intensity of a specific source of pressure in the foreseeable future, I will use three symbols: = for constant, − for declining, and + for growing in strength in the foreseeable future. The symbols are merely an auxiliary to the verbal evaluation.

Column 1: status quo

Existing governments' commitment to existing states is, of course, unquestionable. Whether they are democratically elected or not, the governments' authority, their right to rule, is not questioned by the members of governments. For governments, the full sovereignty of the state and its people is a given that they are understandably reluctant to give up or to negotiate away. The outstanding example is the reluctance of the European governments to renounce sovereignty for a European Community. If we are to assess the probable growth of this source of pressure in the future, I would view it to be constant, and I use the symbol = for this purpose.

Political power used against disintegrative as well as integrative trends will probably grow. By use of political power I refer to legislation, such as the Devolution Bill in Great Britain to contain secessionist/separatist trends and bills in Spain in relation to the Basques and Catalans, and to the use of police force to put down demonstrations and jail leaders, such as in the Philippines, in Ethiopia against the Eritreans, in Nigeria against the Biafrans, and so on. Symbol: +

Recognition of one government by another remains an important element in perpetuating the status quo. Here we ought to include recognition by the United Nations. Note the power of recognition or of the refusal to grant it in the case of the two already "independent Bantustans" in South Africa: the Transkei and Bophuthatswana. Symbol: =

Respect for territorial integrity of existing states and nonintervention in the internal affairs of states are found in the Charter of the United Nations, and official declarations of support abound. The most recent case was the role of the United States in reportedly forcing Somalia to retreat from the Ogaden in the name of respect for the territorial integrity of Ethiopia. Symbol: =

Populations usually support the existence of their own states. Here, however, the question is the intensity of this support as well as the size of the supporting population. Such support varies from time to time and from case to case. In times of war popular support is greater than in times of peace. In some states, such as Sweden, the support is probably greater than in Canada. Although the support is neither constant nor universal, the symbol should probably be: =

The perceived threat to "our" ideological camp by the "other" strongly reinforces the status quo of the modern (nation-)state. The Cold War in the post-World War II period strengthened not only the (nation-)state's territorial and political legitimacy but also the ideological commitment to it. If we assume, as I do, that the Cold War threat will diminish in the future, we ought also assume that its impact on the continuation of the status quo will diminish. The symbol here, considering the future, should probably be: −

By inertia I refer to the acceptance that the state, for good or bad, is here to stay. Briefly, an existing institution is self-perpetuating. The symbol is: =

There is little need to show that academics, in general, perpetuate the status quo in their teaching and writings. The "present" is presented as a logical continuation of the past, and its form is explained, if not justified, in the writings of philosophers from Plato on, in theories of human institutional evolution from the tribe to the state, and so on. That academics holding these views, especially political scientists and historians, teach in educational institutions is in some part responsible for the continuation of the status quo. Nevertheless, academics, in growing numbers and effectiveness, are questioning the appropriateness of the modern (nation-)state to deal with today's problems. In the future I believe this commitment to the status quo will lessen. Therefore, the symbol is: −

Any attempt to sum up these forces must be very crude, for

we have not taken into account the relative weights of the various pressures to each other across the three columns. In my estimation, however, the sources of the pressure for the status quo are either constant or are diminishing in strength. Others, of course, may either evaluate these sources' strengths differently or may add other sources of pressure with various evaluations.

Column 2: the centrifugal trend

It seems to me that the evidence here for growing strength of practically every source of pressure is overwhelming and that the consensus on this point is general.

There is growing recognition of interdependence stemming from increased awareness of the diminution of natural resources. The symbol: +

Awareness of the need for the effective control and regulation of international trade, ecology, and manpower flow is growing and will continue to grow in the foreseeable future. Symbol: +

Governments' interest in economic cooperation is growing in relation to a variety of products: steel, cars, shoes, television sets. Symbol: +

Various utopian ideas and Marxist "internationalism" may be tied together as a visionary view of the future, either in a form of a world government or a world communism. It is difficult to assess the relative strength of these ideas throughout the years, and it is probably fair to assess them as constant: =

Academic literature on the future is growing,[10] but we ought to focus not only on the number of publications, but on the probably widening readership of these publications and on their impact. In any case, it seems that this source of pressure is, or at least will be, growing: +

Column 3: the centripetal trend

What is generally referred to as minority nationalism, subnationalism, or ethnonationalism is proliferating and growing in strength. This source of pressure may prove as strong as the widely recognized pressure toward interdependence. Furthermore, as I stated at the outset, this source of pressure, the main element in the centripetal trend, is reinforced by the centrifugal trend. The symbol here is: +

Another source of pressure toward the centripetal trend is communalism. I refer here not only to the founding of communes, but also to the trend to move toward simpler ways of life, such as the French *autogestion* movement, which, as the term implies, aims at self-development and austere community life. These movements are relevant because in their basic philosophy and approach they question the authority of the sovereign modern state and especially its effectiveness. Although it is difficult to estimate their strength, in my view the prospects for the future are growth and proliferation. Symbol: +

The "withering away" ideology is of course the Marxist notion of the withering away of the state. Although it is shelved in party programs, as an idea for Marxists of various orthodoxy, it cannot be counted dead. Since in my view there is no way of assessing its strength, I prefer to leave its symbol open, undecided.

Extreme-left terrorism, especially the German and Japanese variations, is not yet well understood, but if I read the evidence correctly, one of its motivating forces is the destruction of the existing political, social, and economic institutions of the modern state, not of regimes per se. If this is the case, then they are part of the centripetal trend in the sense of aspiring to the disintegration of modern states from within. If the participants' aim is world communism as an international system, they are part of the centrifugal trend as well. Symbol: +

In sum, in my evaluation, the centripetal forces are gaining relative strength vis-à-vis the status quo, as is the centrifugal trend. That means a growing strength for most of the sources of pressure in both columns 2 and 3. This growth in itself may be slow, and the growth in one column may not necessarily correspond to the growth in the other column, but by their interconnectedness, the two trends will reinforce each other.

ARGUMENT 3: *The centrifugal and centripetal trends reinforce each other.*

The two tendencies complement each other (political fragmentation does not negate economic convergence) and also enhance each other: the greater the political fragmentation, the greater will be the need for economic convergence; the greater the economic convergence, the greater the possibility for political fragmentation. The smaller the political units, especially if economically weaker, the economically more dependent they tend to be, and the greater is their need to join with others for their economic well-being.

Today's small, economically weak, less developed states depend on foreign aid and assistance and tend (or at least often sense themselves) to be subjected to the imperialistic aspirations of stronger states. It is hoped that institutionalized economic relationships among the numerous entities in the less developed states, as well as with the more developed regions of the world, will replace this type of dependence.

The economic weakness and dependence felt on the state level is often greater on the level of the ethnic group that aspires to break away. Prospective economic weakness does *not*, by merely loosening or cutting former ties, necessarily work against the political breakaway tendencies, but, more likely, toward ensuring economic convergence with other political entities. The Quebec separatists, warned of the negative economic consequences of their aim, are likely to attempt to initiate Quebec's economic convergence with truncated Canada and other states rather than retreat from the aim of political independence from Canada.

The greater the prospective economic weakness, the greater will be the trend toward economic convergence; the greater the chances for economic convergence, the greater the tendencies toward political fragmentation. But economic weakness alone is not responsible for the mutual reinforcement of the two trends. The mere complexity of economies, the need for markets, the progress of technology, and the dispersal of raw materials around the world are also potential contributors to the amplification of the simultaneous trends. For example, Great Britain, with a relatively greater diversity of resources, is less inclined to be a full member of an economic system on a continental or wider base than a hypothetically independent Scotland, even if she should own the oil resources in the North Sea. Inversely, a strong continental or wider economic system would move Scotland toward separatism, toward replacing her membership in the British economic system. To take another example, oil-producing Saudi Arabia greatly depends on other resources, be they steel, teachers, food, or cars. The greater the economic convergence in all resources, the greater will be the pressure on Saudi Arabia to share her own resource, reducing her from an economic giant to a small, one-product, sociopolitical system. The greater the trend of economic convergence, the greater the capability to force the one-natural-resource state such as Saudi Arabia to be part of the trend.

ARGUMENT 4: *An alternative system is emerging.*

This argument is probably the most crucial in my presentation. The proposition is that as the complementary centrifugal and centripetal trends reinforce each other against the status quo, they are becoming functionally equivalent to the status quo and, as such, an alternative system to it.

The state is founded on force; it alone claims supreme authority and has acquired unrestricted power over all aspects of public life: social, political, economic, and normative. The centrifugal and centripetal trends challenge *all* aspects of the state monopoly over public life. The centrifugal trend claims for itself the economic and normative functions; the centripetal trend claims the social and political functions. The emerging alternative system is therefore to be composed of a large number of sociopolitical entities interdependent within wider economic-normative entities.

By presenting this alternative system I am not predicting a linear, unidirectional move toward a "new world." The "old world," the present world, with its nuclear threats, international conflicts, and political maneuvering is far too complicated to lend itself to predictions. All I am trying to propose is that the existing, seemingly haphazard pressures against the status quo do form a pattern and do have logical implications. Simply stated, existing pressures (be they secessionist aspirations or regional economic organizations) are undermining the state as a political system, and they carry within themselves a substitute system.

The "new world," the alternative system, is not imminent. I

would, however, warn against overestimating the strength of the modern (nation-)state against the competing trends. We researchers, as liberals educated in the Western world, have learned to regard the modern state as a "natural" framework for human beings, evolved as it has over the centuries. For many of us the future is seen through the prism of the (nation-)state; this prism tends to limit the spectrum of our view. It is true that the modern state is here de jure and de facto, but it is also true that it has not always been here. More than this: I am prepared to argue that the state is a digression, an aberration, founded in many cases as a result of war. But the reasons for the emergence of the state are not our concern here.

What existed before the state is, however, our concern. Without further elaboration, I dare to suggest that the alternative system outlined above is a modern version of types of systems that existed prior to the state. In a forthcoming book I have tried to show that what is unanimously referred to as the traditional West African "kingdom" of Dahomey was not a state as the specialists maintain, but a conglomerate of sociopolitical entities under a ritual head.[11] I would strongly urge researchers to inquire into the pasts of their areas of specialization, where, in my view, they might find the elements of a similar alternative system. Thus, the "new world" is not new at all, but the ancient world in a modern, renewed form. The working of the centrifugal and centripetal trends against the status quo may be seen as the working of social forces or historical forces against the de jure and de facto modern (nation-)state.

The temporariness of the modern state has, of course, been noted by many scholars. Ralph Uwechue, a prominent African intellectual, wrote in an editorial commenting on the lesson of the Bangla Desh secession for Africa:

In Africa and Asia the basic problems posed by the urge for secession are the same. Essentially, it is a queston of precedence between two entities: a piece of territory or a human being. In other words, which should prevail: territorial integrity or fundamental human rights to free political association.[12]

Uwechue also said in the same editorial that "tribes" are in reality nations, and that Africans should try to use the "nation-tribes" as building blocks in an All-African Federation. He dismissed existing political boundaries in Africa: "Are we really right to put faith in the Berlin Charter, which established our present boundaries, and take for an African Bible a document whose stipulations were a mere arrangement of convenience between foreign powers?"[13]

American political scientist Cynthia Enloe writes:

On the one hand, the nation state is indeed a potent political reality; any hypothesis about political behavior that pretended it was merely a chimera would be shallow. On the other hand, nation states are not the sole realities. . . . It is one thing to acknowledge the existence of national policies; it is quite another to assume that they are the logical goal of all political development. Actually, nation states have shown themselves to be fragile and there is no guarantee that their preeminence is any more than a passing phase.[14]

Alfred Cobban, in a book published first in 1945, was even closer to my argument. Cobban said, and I paraphrase him, that self-determination cannot stop at the nation-state; instead, we must think of arrangements that will provide less than absolute sovereignty, arrangements such as sharing of economic units.[15]

Finally, to quote again from Leopold Kohr:

The abandonment of the present large unified-area system of the great powers in favor of a small-state world would not necessarily mean the destruction of all existing kinds of economic unity. . . . *Political* particularism does not automatically entail *economic* particularism.[16]

It is reasonable and legitimate to view the existing world map of (nation-)states as an established reality with great inertial power; it is incorrect to view the boundaries outlined on this map as the permanent framework of peoples' quests for self-determination. Similarly, it is incorrect to view states in their present form as the only possible building blocks of an international system. Unless we contend that the quest of human beings for self-determination has already been satisfied, unless we suppose that present arrangements are the answer to the challenge of economic interdependence, we should admit to the map-changing, structure-changing potential of social, political, economic, and normative pressures.

To summarize:

1. The prevailing views that either we are in the midst of a process toward an integrated world or toward a "balkanized" world are incorrect. The world is moving in two opposite directions: toward economic-normative integration and toward sociopolitical disintegration (from the point of view of the (nation-) state). These two directions are *opposite*, however, only if we take the status quo, the (nation-)state system, as a starting point. If we use the individual human being as the starting point, we may see only one direction: the reintegration of individual human beings into new sociopolitical frameworks, which in turn are reintegrated into wider economic entities.

2. Integration into wider entities is positive only if the issues that we face are in *need* of wider frameworks. Economic and normative issues do seem to need wider frameworks; hence, economic and normative integration is a positive step. But our needs for greater freedom, a more humane environment, a sense of being masters of our own lives, these require smaller entities. Thus, disintegration from the existing political frameworks ought to have positive, not negative connotations.

3. The claim that human evolution is a process of integration from smaller tribal entities into greater ones is only partially true. First of all, in human history many empires have crumbled; there has been possibly as much disintegration as integration. But beyond that, much of political integration has been achieved by the use of force, not by evolution. In any case, it is becoming increasingly evident that the very states that had been the symbols of integration, especially Britain and France, are themselves encountering strong pressures toward sociopolitical disintegration. Integration into wider, bigger, more complex entities is *not* a facet of human evolution.

All of the above leads to a plea for a reevaluation of widely held scholarly views, a reevaluation of what we now believe to be local, temporary, isolated cases of disintegrative trends, and a reevaluation of what we now believe to be a process of integration of (nation-)states into a global world community. The purpose of this chapter has been to stimulate such a reevaluation with the help of the propositions and arguments I have tried to present here. It is also a response to the challenge most recently formulated by a man of the "real world," W. Michael Blumenthal, U.S. secretary of the treasury, in an article in *Foreign Affairs*:

This is a world made up of separate nations, each with its own aspirations, its own history, and its own politics. It is also a world that is shrinking fast, creating new interdependencies and new opportunities. How best can we profit from the benefits of our growing interdependencies while pursuing our separate national needs? That is the basic challenge to which nations must respond.[17]

An answer to these queries has been presented here. If we agree that "nations" are human groups in quest of self-determination, then the answer is that we human beings can profit from the benefits of our growing interdependencies while pursuing our separate needs by creating a large number of "national" sociopolitical frameworks integrated and interdependent in wider, perhaps even global, economic-normative entities. This may not be a perfect world, but it would be the one that responds to the human quest for self-determination in its present phase.

6 A GLIMPSE INTO THE FUTURE

In the preface I wrote that this study was undertaken in order to find a lever in the social sciences. The concept of the quest for self-determination is proposed as such a lever. Defined as the aspiration of human beings to control their own lives, the notion of self-determination may help us to understand some aspects of the past, the present, and the future. In the distant past, human beings were not engaged in a quest for self-determination; in their objective poverty, ignorance, and submission to one or to a few, they thought they had it. In the present, more and more human beings are pursuing self-determination; we live now in the age of self-determination, where more and more human beings are getting the message that they *are* human beings just like others, and are finding even the modern (nation-)state itself an obstacle to the realization of their aspirations. The future, I think, holds a continued quest for self-determination, a continued search for new frameworks. They may not be better than those we now have, but these frameworks will be *deemed* better for a while. And so it might go, ad infinitum.

Is not there a framework or frameworks that can provide self-determination? Perhaps not, but using the lever of self-determina-

tion one may come close to describing it. And now, well aware
of possible criticism from social science colleagues for engaging
in unscientific, unscholarly speculations, I am about to describe
it.

If I am right that the quest for self-determination, the aspiration to rule one's self, is a fundamental human motivation, then
each and every adult human being is, potentially, a kingdom in itself. He or she is the first and ultimate sociopolitical entity, the
ruler and the ruled in one, the object of modernization and development, whatever his or her color, race, religion, height, or intelligence.

This human being is a social animal, in permanent need of
other human beings for his or her physical and mental well-being.
Thomas Hobbes was right when he said that man cannot live alone;
he needs the social framework, the "social contract." Man is said
to enter into a social contract with others, where in return for satisfying his needs in the inevitably coercive framework, he has no
choice but to voluntarily give up his freedom. But there *is* a choice;
there *are* alternatives. The alternatives are scores of sociopolitical
frameworks that man may voluntarily enter and then leave to join
others, be they another family, town, work place, social club, or
political system. Of course, every sociopolitical framework, even
the many alternative ones, is based on coercion, the use of authority and power that results in *objective* limitations on freedom. However, it is not the objective limitations on freedom that motivate
man in quest for self-determination (for being a social animal
means being unfree), but his *subjective* perception of being ruled or
coerced "too much." Such a condition may be corrected by the immediate availability of alternative sociopolitical frameworks that
one may join and leave at will. Sociopolitical entities in turn aggregate into economic-normative framework(s) to coordinate production guided by sets of norms.

Growing economic integration tends toward economic-normative frameworks, which eventually will necessitate the globalization of natural resources—or war—to control inequities stemming
from scarcity. The recognition that this earth's resources belong to
the inhabitants of this earth, to human beings and not to states, is in

its incipient stages now. The centrifugal trend, which includes the rooting of the notion of interdependence, will probably lead to this practical solution.

This, then, is the framework that seems to me to approach a world order where human beings have achieved self-determination: hundreds, maybe thousands of social and political frameworks composed of human beings, all within the economic-normative body that distributes food and energy to all.

Is such a vision realizable? Who knows? Perhaps not. In any case, all available evidence indicates that humanity is very far away from even approximating it. The mere idea of globalization of natural resources, that is, the transfer of ownership of natural resources from states to humanity as a whole, sounds, I admit, simply incredible. We are still in the embryonic stage of analysing north-south relationships, in spite of the fact that the Samozas, the Mobutus, the sheiks who are practically the private owners of states' natural resources are in the south, not in the "rich" north. What are we to do with the notion of hundreds or thousands of political entities, when the nineteenth-century principle of respect for territorial integrity of states still prevails toward the end of the twentieth? How can we conceive of the human being as a kingdom in itself in a world where millions of human beings do not yet themselves know that they *are* human beings and not humble creatures to be used as pawns? How can we seriously relate to visions of a supposedly "good" future in a world where reality is considered inevitable and where might is inescapably right.

It seems to me that the human quest for self-determination is carrying us toward a future like the one I describe here or toward one similar to it. In any event, I have not described a future that I want, but a future that may develop. The seeds of this or a similar future are present all around us, though behind the veil of constitutional political structures, treaty-bound economic patterns, institutional social relations, and codified norms. The present and the seeds of the future are realities. To ignore the former would be naive; to neglect exploration of the latter would be foolish.

NOTES

Chapter 1

1. Alfred Cobban, *The Nation State and National Self-Determination*, (New York: Thomas Y. Crowell Co., 1969), a revised edition of *National Self-Determination* (New York: Oxford University Press, 1945), p. 40.

2. For the legal aspects of the right to self-determination, see A. Rigo Sureda, *The Evolution of the Right to Self-Determination* (Leiden: A. W. Sijthoff, 1973); and Umozurike O. Umozurike, *Self-Determination in International Law* (Hamden, Conn.: Archon Books, 1972).

3. The notion of "activation" as well as the arguments presented here are detailed in chapter 3.

4. The five types are given in detail in chapter 2.

5. A seminal contemporary study of post-World War II Europe is Ernst B. Haas, *The Uniting of Europe: Political, Social, and Economic Forces, 1950–1957.* (Stanford, Calif.: Stanford University Press, 1958, 1968). See also Stanley Hoffmann, "Obstinate or Obsolete? The Fate of the Nation-State and the Case of Western Europe," *Daedalus* 95 (Summer 1966): 867–69.

6. For the use of the expression in this context, see Rupert Emerson, *From Empire to Nation: The Rise to Self-Assertion of Asian and African Peoples* (Boston: Beacon Press, 1962), p. 299; also Kenneth R. Minogue, *Nationalism*, (New York: Basic Books, 1967), p. 137.

7. Daniel Lerner, *The Passing of Traditional Society* (Glencoe, Ill.: Free Press, 1958).

8. Crawford Young, *The Politics of Cultural Pluralism*, (Madison: University of Wisconsin Press, 1976), pp. 527–28.

9. Cobban, *The Nation State and National Self-Determination*, p. 37.

10. Cynthia H. Enloe, *Ethnic Conflict and Political Development*, (Boston: Little, Brown, 1973).

11. I do not mean to say that such attempts by scholars ought not to be made, but that the alternative option ought to be taken into account.

Chapter 2

1. I am referring to the notion of modernization as the primary transmitter of the notion of liberation. See the seminal work of Karl Deutsch, *Nationalism and Social Communication: An Inquiry into the Foundations of Nationality* (Cambridge, Mass.: M.I.T. Press, 1953), which influenced a long list of students of modernization.

2. As noted in *Nationalism: A Report by a Study Group of Members of the Royal Institute of International Affairs* (London: Oxford University Press, 1939), p. 47.

3. Ibid.

4. Walker Connor, "The Politics of Ethnonationalism," *Journal of International Affairs* 27 (1973): 2.

5. George H. Sabine, *A History of Political Theory*, (New York: Henry Holt and Co., 1950), p. 581.

6. Ibid., p. 595.

7. Max Stirner, in K. Lohwith, ed., *Die Hegelische Linke* (Stuttgart: F. Frommann, 1962), p. 69; quoted in Shlomo Avineri, *The Social and Political Thought of Karl Marx* (Cambridge University Press, 1968), p. 45. No less an authority on nationalism than Hans Kohn has stated: "The liberty on which the Declaration [of the Rights of Man and of the Citizen] insisted was personal liberty, not national independence." (*Prelude to Nation-States: The French and German Experience 1789–1815* [Princeton: Van Nostrand, 1967], pp. 3–5). See also Robert A. Nisbet, *The Social Philosophers* (London: Heinemann, 1973), p. 145.

8. The well-known scholar of self-determination Alfred Cobban, after debating at length the issue of the right to self-determination, states: "There is no space here to do more than state, without arguing, my own point of view, which is that rights [to self-determination included] are rights for individual, though not isolated men and women, or they are not rights at all. . . . I should be prepared to reject any theory which asserted the absolute right of the nation, whether to self-determination or to anything else" (*The Nation-State and National Self-Determination* [Crowell, rev. ed., 1969], p. 106).

9. Kohn, *Prelude to Nation-States*, pp. 119–20, emphasis mine.

10. See, for example, Cobban, *The Nation-State and National Self-Determination*, p. 63.

11. Connor gives a different interpretation; see "The Politics of Ethnonationalism," pp. 8–9.

12. Ibid.

13. For example: "Though the French Revolution had little to do with *ethnic* nationalism in terms of principle, it had much to do with it in practice . . . the exhortations of the leaders were soon phrased in *national* and xenophobic terms" (ibid., pp. 6–7; emphasis added).

14. Harold W. V. Temperley, ed., *A History of the Peace Conference of Paris*. Published under the auspices of the Institute of International Affairs (London: H. Frowde, and Hodder & Stoughton, 1920–24), vol. 6, p. 558; the quote is from vol. 1, pp. 398–99.

15. Ray Stannard Baker and William E. Dodd, eds., *War and Peace: Presidential Messages, Addresses, and Public Papers (1917–1924) of Woodrow Wilson* (New York: Harper & Brothers, 1927), vol. 1, pp. 50–51; emphasis added.

16. Ibid., vol. 1, pp. 159–61.

17. A. Rigo Sureda, *The Evolution of the Right to Self-Determination: A Study of United Nations Practice* (Leiden: A. W. Sijthoff, 1973), p. 28, n. 2.

18. G. Murray, "Self-determination of Nationalities," *Journal of the British Institute of International Affairs* 1 (1922): 9; emphasis added; quoted in Rigo Sureda, *The Evolution of the Right to Self-Determination*, p. 95.

19. Cobban, *The Nation State and National Self-Determination*, p. 63.

20. Arno J. Mayer, *Political Origins of the New Diplomacy, 1917–1918* (New Haven: Yale University Press, 1959) uses these terms on p. 333.

21. For example, Lenin's essay from 1916, "The Socialist Revolution and the Right of Nations to Self-Determination," in *The Right of Nations to Self-Determination: Selected Writings by V. I. Lenin* (New York: International Publishers, 1951), pp. 73–85.

22. Arno Mayer, *Political Origins*, p. 382; the Trotsky quote is from *The History of the Russian Revolution*, vol. 1, p. 288.

23. Mayer, *Political Origins*, p. 75.

24. Ibid., pp. 298–99; the phrase "a dominant interest" is from Cobban, *National Self-Determination*, 1945 ed., p. 12.

25. See Lawrence W. Maring, "Woodrow Wilson's Appeals to the People of Europe," *Political Science Quarterly* 74 (December 1959): 498.

26. R. W. van Alstyne, "Woodrow Wilson and the Idea of the Nation State," *International Affairs* 37 (1961): 307.

27. I am focusing on African decolonization. It is to be understood, however, that this form of the quest for self-rule—decolonization—occurred simultaneously in Asia as well. This section was researched and in part written with the cooperation of Ms. Vivienne Kutner, the Hebrew University, Jerusalem.

28. The term is borrowed from Ali Mazrui, *Towards a Pax Africana: A Study of Ideology and Ambition* (Chicago: University of Chicago Press, 1967).

29.   Imanuel Geiss, *The Pan-African Movement* (London: Methuen, 1974), p. 5.

30.   Amy Jacques Garvey, comp., *Philosophy and Opinions of Marcus Garvey: Or, Africa for the Africans*, 2d ed. (London: Frank Cass, 1967), p. 4.

31.   Ibid., p. 71.

32.   George Shepperson, "Notes on Negro American Influences on the Emergence of African Nationalism," in William John Hanna, ed., *Independent Black Africa: The Politics of Freedom* (Chicago: Rand McNally, 1964), pp. 200, 203–4.

33.   J. Ayodele Langley, *Pan-Africanism and Nationalism in West Africa, 1900–1945: A Study in Ideology and Social Classes* (Oxford: Clarendon Press, 1973), p. 117.

34.   D. Clemens, *Yalta* (London: Oxford University Press, 1972, paperback reprint of the 1970 ed.), p. 45. The first three points of the Charter are: "1. Their countries seek no aggrandizement, territorial or other; 2. they desire to see no territorial changes that do not accord with the freely expressed wishes of the people concerned; 3. they respect the right of all peoples to choose the form of government under which they will live" (A. J. P. Taylor, *English History, 1914–1945*, [New York: Oxford University Press, 1965], pp. 559–60.)

35.   Clemens, *Yalta*, p. 297.

36.   As quoted in Umozurike Oji Umozurike, *Self-Determination in International Law* (Hamden, Conn.: Shoe String Press, Archon Book, 1972), p. 188.

37.   Rupert Emerson, *Self-Determination Revisited in the Era of Decolonization*, Harvard University, Center for International Affairs, Occasional Papers, No. 9, December 1964, p. 3.

38.   Ibid., p. 7.

39.   Rupert Emerson, *From Empire to Nation: The Rise to Self-Assertion of Asian and African Peoples* (Boston: Beacon Press, 1960), p. 43.

40.   Leslie Rubin and Brian Weinstein, *Introduction to African Politics: A Continental Approach* (New York: Praeger, 1974), pp. 227–28.

41.   Quoted by David Kimche, *The Afro-Asian Movement: Ideology and Foreign Policy of the Third World* (Jerusalem: Israel University Press, 1973), p. 14, n. 3.

42.   E. M. Hugh-Jones, *Woodrow Wilson and American Liberalism* (London: Hodder and Stoughton Ltd., 1947), p. 247.

43.   Emerson, *From Empire to Nation*, p. 26.

44.   Walker Connor, "Nation-Building or Nation-Destroying?" *World Politics* 24, no. 3 (April 1972): 319.

45.   Pierre L. van den Berghe, "Ethnic Pluralism in Industrial Societies: A Special Case?" *Ethnicity* 3 (1976): 242.

46. Nathan Glazer and Daniel P. Moynihan, eds., *Ethnicity: Theory and Experience* (Cambridge, Mass.: Harvard University Press, 1975), p. 1.

47. Walker Connor, in "Nation-Building or Nation-Destroying?" (p. 320, n. 1), notes two nonrepresentative works of the period: Rupert Emerson's *From Empire to Nation* and Charles W. Anderson, Fred R. von der Mehden, and Crawford Young, *Issues of Political Development* (Englewood Cliffs, N.J.: Prentice-Hall, 1967; 1974).

48. Not least responsible for the rise of "integration" was the American "melting pot" concept, which was ready for exportation together with other products. The Marshall Plan, Truman Doctrine, etc. were also unifying and thus responsible for the "integration" era. We should also mention that there has been a period of decolonization from World War II on, which some might consider basically "disintegrative." It was not, for practically until the eve of the act of independence for many African states in 1960, various formulas were studied for *maintaining* reformed relationships between metropoles and colonies. In the 1958 referendum in French-speaking African colonies, only Guinea chose to break away, while all the others chose to maintain ties with the metropole.

49. Walker Connor, "The Politics of Ethnonationalism," *Journal of International Affairs* 27, no. 1 (1973): 2. The term was first coined by Connor in this article and used again, with further elaboration, in his "Ethnonationalism in the First World: The Present in Historical Perspective," in Milton J. Esman, ed., *Ethnic Conflict in the Western World* (Ithaca N.Y.: Cornell University Press, 1977), pp. 19–45. See also Arnfinn Jorgensen-Dahl, "Forces of Fragmentation in the International System: The Case of Ethnonationalism," *Orbis* 19 (Summer 1975): 652–74.

50. The literature on these and other ethnonationalist cases is voluminous and cannot all be cited here. The cases, apart from the names of the groups involved, may also be found under the headings of subnationalism, ethnic pluralism, ethnic conflict, and nationalism. See, for example, Victor Olorunsola, ed., *The Politics of Cultural Sub-Nationalism* (New York: Doubleday, 1972); Crawford Young, *The Politics of Cultural Pluralism* (Madison: University of Wisconsin Press, 1976); Cynthia Enloe, *Ethnic Conflict and Political Development* (Boston: Little, Brown, 1973).

51. The French Revolution is accepted as a "conventional watershed marking the turn to the age of nationalism," although "a number of nationalist phases and elements can be found far earlier"; cf. Rupert Emerson, *From Empire to Nation*, pp. 188.

52. A persuasive critical view is the work by Cynthia Enloe mentioned above, *Ethnic Conflict and Political Development*. See also Robert A. Packenham, *Liberal America and the Third World: Political Development Ideas in Foreign Aid and Social Science* (Princeton, N. J.: Princeton University Press, 1973).

53. Connor, "Ethnonationalism in the First World," p. 26; Emerson, *From Empire to Nation*, p. 299.

54. See also Abdul A. Said and Luiz R. Simmons, "The Ethnic Factor in World Politics," *Society* 12, no. 2 (January–February 1975): 65–74, and an expanded version under the same title in Said and Simmons, eds., *Ethnicity in an International Context* (New Brunswick, N.J.: Transaction Books, 1976), pp. 15–47. See also Dov Ronen, "Alternative Patterns of Integration in African States," *Journal of Modern African Studies* 14, no. 4 (1976): 577–96; Dov Ronen, "Du conflit de classes au séparatisme ethnique," *Pluriel* 10 (1977): 77–84; Richard D. Lambert, ed., *Ethnic Conflict in the World Today*, September 1977 issue of the *Annals of the American Academy of Political and Social Science*.

55. For various definitions of ethnicity, see Wsewolod W. Isajiw, "Definitions of Ethnicity," *Ethnicity* 1 (1974): 111–24. See also Daniel Bell's convincing argument on the relationship between ethnicity and politics in "Ethnicity and Social Change," in Glazer and Moynihan, *Ethnicity*, pp. 140–74.

56. See n. 49 and Connor's "Nation-Building or Nation-Destroying?"

57. Professor Connor was kind enough to read and comment on a draft of this chapter. His comments were taken into account to provide, to the best of my judgment, a correct interpretation of his views on ethnonationalism. He should, of course, in no way be held responsible either for my interpretation or for my elaboration of the thesis on ethnonationalism.

58. "Ethnonationalism in the First World," p. 23.

59. "The Politics of Ethnonationalism," p. 2.

60. Ibid., p. 1.

61. "Ethnonationalism in the First World," p. 23.

62. "The Politics of Ethnonationalism," p. 20. The scholarly works that Connor refers to consider ethnic unrest a disturbing and/or destabilizing phenomenon which is to be "solved," "regulated," "managed," "controlled," etc. See Eric A. Nordlinger, *Conflict Regulation in Divided Societies*, Harvard University, Center for International Affairs, Occasional Papers in International Affairs, No. 29, January 1972; Young, *The Politics of Cultural Pluralism*; Alvin Rabushka and K. A. Shepsle, *Politics in Plural Societies: A Theory of Democratic Instability* (Columbus, Ohio: Charles E. Merrill, 1972); Donald Rothchild, "The Politics of African Separatism," *Journal of International Affairs* 15 (1961): 18–28, to mention only a few.

63. "The Politics of Ethnonationalism," p. 2, n. 4.

64. Ibid., p. 2.

65. Ibid., n. 4.

66. This appears to be a tautology, which is a critical point in Connor's definition.

67.   I relegate the pursuit of this important question to the footnote because it is not a major point in my argument. There are several issues,
however:
    1. Can one speak of "unity of race" in the twentieth century, not be-
cause *race* is a word out of fashion, but because unity of race (maybe even
of culture) hardly exists any more in its "pristine form"?
    2. What is the "basic" human category of, for example, the Hungarian
peasant migrating to the United States? May he be a member of another human category? In sum, can any objective category be relevant other than in
pure scientific terms when social, political, and economic interactions are
as much, or more, motivated by perceptions, impressions, feelings, ideas,
and the like? Basic human categories may very well be *socially* irrelevant.
With the advent of sociobiology, this notion may have to be redefined, but
in the meantime, I see only two basic human categories: the individual and
humanity as a whole (chapter 3). For comments of sociobiology, see
Edward O. Wilson, *Sociobiology: A New Synthesis* (Cambridge, Mass.:
Harvard University Press, 1975); and Pierre L. van den Berghe, *Man in
Society: A Biosocial View* (New York: Elsevier, 1975).
    68.   See Young, *The Politics of Cultural Pluralism*, p. 461; also Simon
Ottenberg, "Ibo Receptivity to Change," in William R. Bascom and
Melville J. Herskovits, eds., *Continuity and Change in African Cultures*
(Chicago: University of Chicago Press, 1959).
    69.   Young, *The Politics of Cultural Pluralism*, chapters 8 and 12.
    70.   Eritrean heterogeneity is made up of: Arab/Beja, Arab/Afar, black
African, and Christian plateau dwellers.
    71.   Milton J. Esman, "Scottish Nationalism, North Sea Oil, and the
British Response," in Esman, *Ethnic Conflict in the Western World*, p.
278.
    72.   Young, *The Politics of Cultural Pluralism*, pp. 489–90.
    73.   The Basque language is unrelated to any of the Indo-European lan-
guages; the Basques have the highest incidence of the Rh negative blood
factor of any population in the world. Davydd J. Greenwood, "Continuity
in Change: Spanish Basque Ethnicity as a Historical Process," in Esman,
Ethnic Conflict in the Western World, p. 84.
    74.   Pierre van den Berghe, "Ethnic Pluralism in Industrial Societies: A
Special Case?" pp. 243–44. See also Young, *The Politics of Cultural Pluralism*, p. 41.
    75.   These will be referred to and classified subsequently.
    76.   In interviews conducted by the author in Western Nigeria among
Christian Yoruba in 1967, many expressed uneasiness about Western
Nigeria's siding with the North against the East, and not vice versa. For a
contemporary analysis, see S. K. Panter-Brick, "The Right to Self-Determination: Its Application to Nigeria," *International Affairs* 44 (April 1968),
especially p. 262.

77. Ross K. Baker, "The Emergence of Biafra: Balkanization or Nation-Building?" *Orbis* 12, no. 1 (Spring 1968): 530.

78. The argument is stated in his article "Nation-Building or Nation-Destroying?" See also Connor's "Ethnonationalism in the First World," p. 20.

79. "Nation-Building or Nation-Destroying?" pp. 330–31.

80. Ibid.; also quoted in his "Ethnonationalism in the First World," p. 28.

81. "Nation-Building or Nation-Destroying?" p. 331. In Connor's article entitled "The Political Significance of Ethnonationalism within Western Europe," in Said and Simmons, eds., *Ethnicity in an International Context*, there is a different version: "Any people, simply because it considers itself to be a separate national group, is uniquely and exclusively qualified to determine its own political status, including, should it so desire, the right to its own state" (p. 112).

82. "Nation-Building or Nation-Destroying?" p. 331.

83. "The Politics of Ethnonationalism," pp. 3–4.

84. "Ethnonationalism in the First World," p. 33.

85. Michael Hechter, *Internal Colonialism* (Berkeley: University of California Press, 1975).

Chapter 3

1. In my research on this subject I have looked through some of the literature on "man in nature," "primitive man," "tradition," and "traditionalism," from Plato through Marx, Max Weber, the anthropological literature, and the literature on "modernization." My conclusion is that what I would call classic functional aggregations—tribes, primitive societies—are defined "objectively" in the literature (i.e., from the outsider's point of view) according to the standards of the ideal or modern or technologically developed sociopolitical frameworks. Plato looks at them from the point of view of an objectively defined ideal system, Max Weber from the point of view of the capitalist system, Marx from the point of view of a preferable use of the means of production, Apter and others from the point of view of modernity. I do not quarrel with their definitions from *these* points of view; I merely emphasize what I believe to be the *subjective* view of members of functional aggregations. They think themselves masters of their own lives. Max Weber, for example, explains "traditionalism": "A man does not 'by nature' wish to earn more and more money, but simply to live as he is accustomed to live and to earn as much as is necessary for that purpose" (*The Protestant Ethic and the Spirit of Capitalism*, translated by Talcott Parsons [London: George Allen and Unwin, 1930], p. 60). Marx, referring to India as the archetype of oriental despotism, speaks of "idyllic villages," each of which forms a "little world in itself" and is

nondialectical, i.e., does not have impetus for change. For an analysis, see Shlomo Avineri, *Karl Marx on Colonialism and Modernization* (New York: Anchor Books, Doubleday, 1969).

Robert A. Nisbet observes, "Western philosophy, as we know it, begins with the fall of the kinship community in ancient Athens." It was Cleisthenes in 509 B.C. who "instigated reforms . . . leading to the annihilation of the tribes, phratries, and clans under which the Athenians had lived for centuries." It is possible that what Nisbet refers to as the quest for community as the main line of history is the quest for kinship community. But quest is for the kinship community, not because it is the organic human entity, but because the individual has historically found in *it* the subjective freedom, the self-determination, that he seeks. The work of Nisbet I am referring to is *The Social Philosophers*, (London: Heinemann, 1974); the quote is from page 3.

2. An insightful study of this change of identity is Crawford Young's *The Politics of Cultural Pluralism* (Madison: University of Wisconsin in Press, 1976).

3. Robert A. Nisbet, *The Quest for Community* (New York: Oxford University Press, 1953), p. 115.

4. Young, *The Politics of Cultural Pluralism*, pp. 12–13.

5. Nisbet, *The Quest for Community*, p. 75.

Chapter 4

1. For this section on Scotland, the following sources in particular were used: James G. Kellas, *The Scottish Political System* (Cambridge: The University Press, 1973); James G. Kellas, *Modern Scotland* (London: Pall Mall, 1968); H. J. Hanham, *Scottish Nationalism* (Cambridge, Mass.: Harvard University Press, 1969); Michael Hechter, *Internal Colonialism* (Berkeley: University of California Press, 1975); Milton J. Esman, "Scottish Nationalism, North Sea Oil, and the British Response," in Milton J. Esman, ed., *Ethnic Conflict in the Western World* (Ithaca, N. Y.: Cornell University Press, 1977).

2. Esman, "Scottish Nationalism," p. 261.

3. Kellas, *The Scottish Political System*, p. 137.

4. Esman, "Scottish Nationalism," p. 284.

5. Ibid., p. 273.

6. This view was expressed by the SNP representative in an interview in Cambridge, Mass., 18 March 1977.

7. Norman Buch in *The Times* (London), 4 November 1975.

8. Esman, "Scottish Nationalism," p. 281.

9. An editorial in *The Times* (London), 24 October 1975, noted: "Most Scots remain against a raw policy of separation and the break-up of the United Kingdom, but the shift in Scottish politics towards a Scottish

Assembly and substantial devolution of power from Whitehall is treading towards the nationalist line.''

10. Among the sources on Nigeria, the following items were especially useful: Walter Schwarz, *Nigeria* (New York: Praeger, 1968); A. H. M. Kirk-Greene, *Crisis and Conflict in Nigeria* (London: Oxford University Press, 1971); Robert Melson and Howard Wolpe, eds., *Nigeria: Modernization and the Politics of Communalism* (East Lansing: Michigan State University Press, 1971); Robin Luckham, *The Nigerian Military: A Sociological Analysis of Authority and Revolt, 1960–67* (Cambridge: The University Press, 1971).

11. For an evaluation of the two coups, see Dov Ronen, ''Alternative Patterns of Integration in African States,'' *Journal of Modern African Studies* 14, no. 4 (1976): 584.

12. Luckham, *The Nigerian Military*, p. 17.

13. Ibid., p. 58.

14. Young, *The Politics of Cultural Pluralism*, p. 471.

15. Luckham, *The Nigerian Military*, p. 67.

16. After Nigeria was declared a unitary state, military governors were appointed to the former regions.

17. Luckham, *The Nigerian Military*, p. 68.

18. Ibid., p. 324; emphasis mine.

19. Ibid.; emphasis in the original.

20. Pierre van den Berghe, ''Nigeria and Peru: Two Contrasting Cases in Ethnic Pluralism,'' mimeo, 1977, p. 7.

21. This case is treated analytically and without reference to the ongoing political debates (as are all the others). I chose this example because the issue is known and is actual. Whether the Palestinian identity is to be politically recognized or not is not my primary concern here.

22. Among the various sources I studied, the following are quoted or were especially useful: Jon Kimche, *The Second Arab Awakening* (New York: Holt, Rinehart and Winston, 1970); Joel Carmichael, *The Shaping of the Arabs: A Study in Ethnic Identity* (New York: Macmillan, 1967); John Marlowe, *Arab Nationalism and British Imperialism: A Study in Power Politics* (New York: Praeger, 1961); Y. Harkabi, *Palestinians and Israel* (New York: Wiley, 1974); George Antonius, *The Arab Awakening: The Story of the Arab National Movement* (London: Hamish Hamilton, 1938); and David C. Gordon, *Self-Determination and History in the Third World* (Princeton, N.J.: Princeton University Press, 1971); Jacob Hurewitz, *The Struggle for Palestine* (New York: Norton, 1950); Walter Z. Laqueur, *A History of Zionism* (New York: Schocken Books, 1976).

23. The Arab-Zionist/colonialism syndrome is evident in practically every book on the subject prior to, and to an extent after, 1967. Israel was presented to the Arab world as a branch of European colonialism. David C. Gordon notes that in the Arab history and civics course texts used in United

Nations Relief and Works Agency schools in Israeli-occupied territories after the 1967 war, Arabism was pictured as confronted with imperialism and Zionism. This was the finding of a "Commission of Outside Experts" of UNRWA-UNESCO. See also Arnold Hottinger, *The Arabs: Their History, Culture and Place in the Modern World* (Berkeley: University of California Press, 1963).

24. Jon Kimche observes, "Within a week of the end of the war in June 1967 there had come the first significant move towards the establishment of a Palestinian Arab nation since the early days of British mandatory rule" (*The Second Arab Awakening*, p. 251).

25. Among the many books on South Africa, the following were particularly helpful: Heribert Adam, ed., *South Africa: Sociological Perspectives* (London: Oxford University Press, 1971); Heribert Adam, *Modernizing Racial Domination: South Africa's Political Dynamics* (Berkeley: University of California Press, 1971); Gwendolen M. Carter, *The Politics of Inequality: South Africa since 1948* (New York: Octagon, 1977, reprint of 1958 ed.); Gwendolen M. Carter and Patrick O'Meara, eds., *Southern Africa in Crisis* (Bloomington: Indiana University Press, 1977); Edward Feit, *Urban Revolt in South Africa, 1960–1964* (Evanston, Ill.: Northwestern University Press, 1971); A. Keppel-Jones, *South Africa: A Short History* (London: Hutchinson University Library, 1975); Leo Kuper, *Passive Resistance in South Africa* (New Haven: Yale University Press, 1957); Pierre L. van den Berghe, *South Africa: A Study in Conflict* (Berkeley: University of California Press, 1975); Edward Roux, *Time Longer than Rope: A History of the Black Man's Struggle for Freedom in South Africa* (Madison: University of Wisconsin Press, 1964).

26. There was, of course, opposition to oppression, discrimination, and white racism. The opposition in South Africa, institutionalized by the founding of the African National Congress (ANC) in 1912, may possibly be drawn as a parallel to the Pan-African phase in the black African quest for self-determination (chapter 2). Here the dominant resistance focused on particular acts and their discriminatory implications: the ratification of the Constitution of South Africa in 1909, the Natives Land Act of 1913, and so forth. Again, the aim was to obtain more rights, more liberal laws for blacks. The case in point is the split in the ANC in 1935 on whether or not to support the Natives' Representative Council and thus cooperate with the government in order to obtain more rights.

27. For the role of the South African Communist party, see, among others, Feit, *Urban Revolt in South Africa 1960–1964*, especially pp. 278–300, and E. Roux, *Time Longer than Rope*.

28. Aristide R. Zolberg, "Les Nationalismes et le nationalisme québécois," *Choix: Le Nationalisme québécois à la croisée des chemins* (Quebec: Université Laval, Centre québécois de relations internationales, 1975), p. 50.

Chapter 5

1.   By structural change is meant change in boundaries, institutions, units in a state or in the international system, such as the change from unitary to federal system in a state, or a change from the present international system to, say, world government. Structural change is specfically distinguished from regime change, such as from civilian to military, ideological shifts, such as from socialism to free enterprise, and the like.

2.   One ought not to attach too much importance to the appropriateness of these labels. They are used here primarily for reference. I also considered using the dichotomies: distintegration-integration, as well as fragmentation-convergence, instead of centripetal-centrifugal, alongside the "status quo" label. The last pair is used here because I found it appropriate to present the trends from the point of view of the individual human being: the first trend moves toward the individual as the center (centripetal); in the second trend the individual continues to be a member of the state ("status quo"); the third trend moves away from the individual as the center (centrifugal).

3.   The four terms—economic, political, social, and normative—allude here to the four Parsonian subsystems. Although there will be no further reference to Talcott Parsons, the indirect reference to his conceptual framework will be recognized.

Briefly, to simplify, if not vulgarize the Parsonian scheme: In every state there are four forces (and institutions, processes): economic—concerns production; political—concerns allocation (of goods/production); social—concerns the social glue among human beings; and normative—concerns the norms and values that influence our attitude toward other human beings. The modern (nation-)state encompasses all four subsystems; the individual citizen is (expected to be) a member in each of the four subsystems of the particular state in which he is a citizen. Thus he or she produces for the state (contributes to the gross national product, pays taxes, etc.); is allocated goods and services by the state (by the decision makers in whose election he or she usually participates); interacts with other citizens of the same state, thus forming voluntary associations and ultimately a nation; and respects the laws, regulations, and values of his or her state and has a sense of solidarity with the cocitizens.

The first point maintains that the centripetal trend tends to encompass the social and political subsystems; the centrifugal trend tends to encompass the economic and normative subsystems.

4.   A similar idea is persuasively presented in Leopold Kohr, *The Breakdown of Nations* (New York: Rinehart, 1957). Kohr suggests, "There seems only one cause behind all forms of social misery: *bigness* [of states]" (p. ix). He questions the utility of social, cultural, economic reforms within the state and proposes, instead, cutting them in size, what I

have called structural change. I am indebted to Professor Edward Tiryakian for drawing my attention to this thought-provoking work.

5. Only a preliminary view is presented here. Hence, the discussion is brief and footnotes kept to a minimum.

6. This argument is possibly supported by the thesis of the sociobiologists. See Edward O. Wilson, *Sociobiology: A New Synthesis* (Cambridge, Mass.: Harvard University Press, 1975); and Pierre van den Berghe, *Man in Society: A Bio-social View* (New York: Elsevier, 1975).

7. Ernst B. Haas, "The Uniting of Europe and the Uniting of Latin America," *Journal of Common Market Studies* 5/4 (1967): 322.

8. Reginald H. Green and Anne Seidman, *Unity or Poverty: The Economics of Pan-Africanism* (Baltimore: Penguin, 1968).

9. Anthony H. Birch, "Minority Nationalist Movements and Theories of Political Integration," *World Politics* 30/3 (1978): 341–44.

10. James P. Sewell, *World Order Studies: A Critical Examination* (Princeton, N.J.: Princeton University Center for International Studies, 1974). Sewell lists future world order studies under twelve headings, each of them covering numerous publications (pp. 9 ff.). For another spectrum of views on future world orders, see especially the "Editor's Report" in Stanley Hoffmann, ed., *Conditions of World Order* (Boston: Houghton Mifflin, 1968). See also Richard A. Falk, *A Study of Future Worlds* (New York: Free Press, 1975); Louis R. Beres and Harry R. Targ, *Constructing Alternative World Futures: Reordering the Planet* (Cambridge, Mass.: Schenkman, 1977); Saul H. Mendlovitz, ed., *On the Creation of a Just World Order: Preferred Worlds for the 1990's* (New York: Free Press, 1975).

11. Dov Ronen, *In Search of the "State" in Pre-Colonial Africa* (London: Frank Cass, forthcoming).

12. Ralph Uwechue, "From Tribe to Nation," *Africa* 7 (1972): 12.

13. Ibid.

14. Cynthia H. Enloe, *Ethnic Conflict and Political Development* (Boston: Little, Brown, 1973), p. 11.

15. Alfred Cobban, *The Nation State and National Self-Determination* (New York: Crowell, 1969), pp. 129, 143–44, 259.

16. Kohr, *Breakdown of Nations*, pp. 166–67.

17. W. Michael Blumenthal, "Steering in Crowded Waters," *Foreign Affairs* 56, no. 4 (July 1978): 739.

Selected Bibliography

This is not a comprehensive bibliography but a short list of some materials that have stimulated my thinking on the subject.

Akzin, Benjamin. *State and Nation*. London: Hutchinson, 1964.

Avineri, Shlomo, ed. *Karl Marx on Colonialism and Modernization*. Garden City, N.Y.: Doubleday, 1968.

————. *The Social and Political Thought of Karl Marx*. London: Cambridge University Press, 1968.

Baker, Ross K. "The Emergence of Biafra: Balkanization or Nation-Building?" *Orbis* 12/1 (Spring 1968).

Bay, Christian. *The Structure of Freedom*. New York: Atheneum, 1965.

Berman, Marshall. *The Politics of Authenticity: Radical Individualism and the Emergence of Modern Society*. New York: Atheneum, 1970.

Birch, Anthony H. "Minority Nationalist Movements and Theories of Political Integration." *World Politics* 30/3 (1978).

Bozeman, Adda B. *Conflict in Africa: Concepts and Realities*. Princeton, N.J.: Princeton University Press, 1976.

Buchheit, Lee C. *Secession: The Legitimacy of Self-Determination*. New Haven, Conn.: Yale University Press, 1978.

Carr, Edward H. *The Bolshevik Revolution: 1917–1923*. Baltimore: Penguin Books, 1966.

Cobban, Alfred. *The Nation State and National Self-Determination*. New York: Thomas Y. Crowell, 1969.

Connor, Walker. "Nation-Building or Nation-Destroying?" *World Politics* 24/3 (April 1972).

————. "The Politics of Ethnonationalism." *Journal of International Affairs* 27/1 (1973).

135

Deutsch, Karl W. *Nationalism and Social Communication: An Inquiry into the Foundations of Nationality*. Cambridge, Mass.: M.I.T. Press, 1953.

Emerson, Rupert. *From Empire to Nation: The Rise to Self-Assertion of Asian and African Peoples*. Cambridge, Mass.: Harvard University Press, 1960.

―――. *Self-Determination Revisited in the Era of Decolonization*. Cambridge, Mass.: Center for International Affairs, Harvard University, 1964. C.F.I.A. Occasional Papers, No. 9.

Enloe, Cynthia H. *Ethnic Conflict and Political Development*. Boston: Little, Brown, 1973.

Esman, Milton J., ed. *Ethnic Conflict in the Western World*. Ithaca, N.Y.: Cornell University Press, 1977.

Falk, Richard A. *A Study of Future Worlds*. New York: Free Press, 1975.

Fanon, Frantz. *The Wretched of the Earth*. New York: Grove Press, 1963.

Geiss, Imanuel. *The Pan-African Movement*. London: Methuen, 1974.

Gordon, David C. *Self-Determination and History in the Third World*. Princeton, N.J.: Princeton University Press, 1971.

Hechter, Michael. *Internal Colonialism: The Celtic Fringe in British National Development, 1536–1966*. Berkeley: University of California Press, 1975.

Hoffmann, Stanley, ed. *Conditions of World Order*. Boston: Houghton Mifflin, 1968.

Horowitz, Donald. "Three Dimensions of Ethnic Politics." *World Politics* 23/2 (January 1971).

Hugh-Jones, Edward M. *Woodrow Wilson and American Liberalism*. London: Hodder & Stoughton, 1947.

Huntington, Samuel P. *Political Order in Changing Societies*. New Haven: Yale University Press, 1968.

Isajiw, Wsewolod W. "Definitions of Ethnicity." *Ethnicity* 1 (1974).

Jorgensen-Dahl, Arnfinn. "Forces of Fragmentation in the International System: The Case of Ethnonationalism." *Orbis* 19 (Summer 1975).

Kedourie, Elie, ed. *Nationalism in Asia and Africa*. London: Weidenfeld and Nicolson, 1970.

Kohn, Hans. *Prelude to Nation States: The French and German Experience, 1789–1815*. Princeton, N. J.: Van Nostrand, 1967.

Kohr, Leopold. *The Breakdown of Nations*. New York: Rinehart, 1957.

Lambert, Richard D., ed. *Ethnic Conflict in the World Today*. Philadelphia: American Academy of Political and Social Science, 1977. (Its Annals, vol. 433).

Langley, J. Ayodele. *Pan-Africanism and Nationalism in West Africa, 1900–1945: A Study in Ideology and Social Classes*. Oxford: Clarendon Press, 1973.

Lenin, V. I. *The Right of Nations to Self-Determination* . New York: International Publishers, 1951.

Lijphart, A. "Consociational Democracy." *World Politics* 21/2 (January 1969).

Melson, Robert, and Wolpe, Howard, eds. *Nigeria: Modernization and the Politics of Communalism*. East Lansing: Michigan State University Press, 1971.

Mendlovitz, Saul H., ed. *On the Creation of a Just World Order: Preferred Worlds for the 1990's*. New York: Free Press, 1975.

Moore, Barrington, Jr. *Social Origins of Dictatorship and Democracy: Lord and Peasant in the Making of the Modern World*. Boston: Beacon Press, 1966.

Nationalism: A Report by a Study Group of Members of the Royal Institute of International Affairs. London: Oxford University Press, 1939.

Nisbet, Robert A. *The Quest for Community: A Study in the Ethics of Order and Freedom*. New York: Oxford University Press, 1953.

————. *The Social Philosophers: Community and Conflict in Western Thought*. London: Heinemann, 1974.

Nozick, Robert. *Anarchy, State and Utopia*. New York: Basic Books, 1974.

Nordlinger, Eric A. *Conflict Regulation in Divided Societies*. Cambridge, Mass.: Center for International Affairs, Harvard University, 1972. C.F.I.A. Occasional Papers, No. 29.

Panter-Brick, S. K. "The Right to Self-Determination: Its Application to Nigeria." *International Affairs* 44 (April 1968).

Rigo Sureda, A. *The Evolution of the Right to Self-Determination: A Study of United Nations Practice*. Leiden: A. W. Sijthoff, 1973.

Ronen, Dov. "Alternative Patterns of Integration in African States." *Journal of Modern African Studies* 14/4 (1976).

————. "Du Conflit de classes au séparatisme ethnique." *Pluriel* 10 (1977).

Rothchild, Donald S. "The Politics of African Separatism." *Journal of International Affairs* 15 (1961).

Sabine, George H. *A History of Political Theory*. New York: Holt, 1950.

Shaheen, Samad. *The Communist (Bolshevik) Theory of National Self-Determination: Its Historical Evolution up to the October Revolution*. The Hague: W. van Hoeve, 1956.

Snyder, Louis L. *The Meaning of Nationalism*. New York: Greenwood Press, 1968.

Stalin, Joseph. *Marxism and the National Question*. New York: International Publishers, 1942.

Temperley, Harold W. V., ed. *A History of the Peace Conference of Paris*. Published under the auspices of the Institute of International Affairs. London: H. Frowde, and Hodder & Stoughton, 1920–24. 6 vols.

Toffler, Alvin. *Future Shock*. New York: Random House, 1970.

Umozurike, Umozurike Oji. *Self-Determination in International Law*.

Hamden, Conn.: Archon Books, 1972.

van Alstyne, R. W. "Woodrow Wilson and the Idea of the Nation State." *International Affairs* 37 (1961).

van den Berghe, Pierre L. "Ethnic Pluralism in Industrial Societies: A Special Case?" *Ethnicity* 3 (1976).

———, and Brass, Paul. "Ethnicity and Nationalism in World Perspective." *Ethnicity* 3 (1976).

van Dyke, Vernon. "Human Rights and the Rights of Groups." *American Journal of Political Science* 18/4 (1974).

———. "Self-Determination and Minority Rights." *International Studies Quarterly* 13/3 (1969).

Young, Crawford. *The Politics of Cultural Pluralism*. Madison: University of Wisconsin Press, 1976.

INDEX